Social Science
And National Policy

Trans-**action** Books

Social Science
And National Policy

Edited by
FRED R. HARRIS

Trans-**action** Books

Published and distributed by
Aldine Publishing Company

The essays in this book originally appeared
in *Trans-action* Magazine

309.173
H 31a

MN

Contents

Preface

However diverse their attitudes and interpretations may sometimes be, social scientists are now entering a period of shared realization that the United States—both at home and abroad—has entered a crucial period of transition. Indeed, the much burdened word "crisis" has now become a commonplace among black militants, Wall Street lawyers, housewives, and even professional politicians.

For the past six years, *Trans*-action magazine has dedicated itself to the task of reporting the strains and conflicts within the American system. But the magazine has done more than this. It has pioneered in social programs for changing the society, offered the kind of analysis that has permanently restructured the terms of the "dialogue" between peoples and publics, and offered the sort of prognosis that makes for real alterations in social and political policies directly affecting our lives.

The work done in the pages of *Trans*-action has crossed

disciplinary boundaries. This represents much more than simple cross-disciplinary "team efforts." It embodies rather a recognition that the social world cannot be easily carved into neat academic disciplines. That, indeed, the study of the experience of blacks in American ghettos, or the manifold uses and abuses of agencies of law enforcement, or the sorts of overseas policies that lead to the celebration of some dictatorships and the condemnation of others, can best be examined from many viewpoints and from the vantage points of many disciplines.

This series of books clearly demonstrates the superiority of starting with real world problems and searching out practical solutions, over the zealous guardianship of professional boundaries. Indeed, it is precisely this approach that has elicited enthusiastic support from leading American social scientists for this new and dynamic series of books.

The demands upon scholarship and scientific judgment are particularly stringent, for no one has been untouched by the current situation. Each essay republished in these volumes bears the imprint of the author's attempt to communicate his own experience of the crisis. Yet, despite the sense of urgency these papers exhibit, the editors feel that many have withstood the test of time, and match in durable interest the best of available social science literature. This collection of *Trans*-action articles, then, attempts to address itself to immediate issues without violating the basic insights derived from the classical literature in the various fields of social science.

The subject matter of these books concerns social changes that have aroused the long-standing needs and present-day anxieties of us all. These changes are in organizational life styles, concepts of human ability and intelligence, changing patterns of norms and morals, the relationship of social conditions to physical and biological environments, and in the status of social science with national policy making.

This has been a decade of dissident minorities, massive shifts in norms of social conduct, population explosions and urban expansions, and vast realignments between nations of the world. The social scientists involved as editors and authors of this *Trans*-action series have gone beyond observation of these critical areas, and have entered into the vital and difficult tasks of explanation and interpretation. They have defined issues in a way making solutions possible. They have provided answers as well as asked the right questions. Thus, this series should be conceived as the first collection dedicated not to the highlighting of social problems alone, but to establishing guidelines for social solutions based on the social sciences.

THE EDITORS
Trans-action

A Strategy For the Social Sciences

FRED R. HARRIS

"One small step for man—one giant leap for mankind." The words of astronaut Neil Armstrong will resound throughout the world as man and mankind move forward to meet the challenges of the last third of the twentieth century. The mobilization of scientific and technological resources has resulted in the achievement of fantastic feats, many of which, until the recent past, belonged in the realm of science fiction. The spectacular technological progress of America's space program together with the psychological uplifting that the moon landing has engendered makes timely a rededication of national will to alleviate and eradicate the social problems that plague the planet earth.

Man has escaped the earth's gravity but seemingly cannot escape the forces of conflict and turmoil that beset the world. Perhaps he will now gain a broader perspective of the difficult job ahead and more clearly see the urgency for developing a national strategy for the social sciences,

1

keeping in mind the hope of following the dictum of Alexander Pope, "The proper study of mankind is man." The space program can be considered to have placed in sharper contrast the difference between what man can do and what he should do. The challenges for social scientists, though no less complex than before, are now more visible.

If man has a more sharply defined role in history and the unfolding of history is thereby altered in part, then the social sciences should be placed in an elevated position in order to make a more decisive impact on the future. A national strategy for the social sciences is a prerequisite for marshalling the resources necessary for attacking the divisive forces that tend to tear apart the fabric of American democracy.

The social sciences have evolved more recently, and in a manner not entirely similar to their cousins, the natural sciences. While the latter have grown up from what was once, until the 17th and 18th centuries, the all-encompassing field of natural philosophy, the social sciences have been influenced by both the natural sciences and the humanities. Though the social sciences owe much to the natural sciences, they have certainly not been wholly dependent on them for their development, contrary to what many contend. And it is rather presumptuous to suggest that the social sciences should emulate the natural sciences in matters of methodology, technique and style. The social sciences should draw on that part of their heritage derived from the humanities as much as on that taken from the natural sciences in order that relevancy not be sacrificed for the sake of rigor.

During the days of the New Deal the social sciences, particularly economics, were elevated to a position of high status vis-à-vis the natural sciences. In fact, in 1935, President Roosevelt established the National Resources Board which in turn set up a science committee which recognized the fields of social science and education as co-equals with the natural sciences. Underscoring this relative prominence of the social sciences are statistics showing that in 1938 the social sciences received 24 percent of total government expenditures for research. By 1950 this had diminished to about 8 percent, and for the last ten years the social sciences have been allocated between only $3\frac{1}{2}$ and 5 percent of federal funds for research.

The short-lived modicum of prestige was quickly eclipsed by the rapid rise in stature of the natural sciences. To an extent this was a result of eye-catching and breathtaking accomplishments such as the development of the atomic bomb, radar and the proximity fuse, which were influential in winning World War II. The natural sciences maintained this well-deserved image throughout the Cold War era; only as the icy relations between East and West began to thaw did the natural sciences tend to lose some of their status. All the while the social sciences remained in the penumbra of their older and richer cousins, receiving less attention and consideration. Consequently, solutions to social as compared to scientific problems experienced a similar fate.

The growing social pressures brought on by the civil rights revolution and followed by the declaration of war on poverty had the earmarks of a national strategy, but there was no follow-up "Manhattan Project" for the social sciences. This gave greater cogency to the argument that the social sciences had still not been accorded the recognition they deserved in our system of national priorities. Insufficient priority implies lack of visibility, status and prestige, which in turn tends to lessen the credibility of the social sciences. The intensity and urgency of problems identified by social science research and solutions shaped and designed by social scientists will not be appreciated if governmental structures and programs for supporting the social sciences are inadequate.

A strategy for the social sciences can come about only when the intensity of social problems, the urgency of related solutions and the relevancy of supporting mechanisms are closely linked together. This coupling process can result from sharp public debate that, for example, identifies programs that should be implemented and institutions that should be created. By the use of various forums such debate and dialogue can shape and fashion the goals, priorities, and policies that are necessary for the development of a national strategy for the social sciences.

The selection of recent articles which originally appeared in *Trans*-action (a journal that exemplifies the type of forum previously referred to) is arranged in three categories: social problems, proposed solutions, and mechanisms. The nature of the interrelationships among the three will ultimately determine the effectiveness of a national strategy.

The book, due to obvious page limitations, is not a definitive work, and the selections do not cover the panoply of problems and issues besetting the nation. A complete and comprehensive coverage would, in scope and magnitude, appear like a modern version of Diderot's *Encyclopédie*. Yet, the articles are representative of a pervasive major theme—the role of the social sciences in the alleviation and elimination of poverty. On the one hand, poverty is surrounded by a sea of concepts and processes—urbanization, alienation, frustration, violence, law and order, repression, permissiveness, justice, acculturation, rural deterioration, rural-to-urban population shift, malnutrition, underclass, and so forth. On the other hand, the social sciences, if nurtured and carefully guided in light of their fragility and sensitivity and their incisiveness, can serve to illuminate social problems and develop the requisite tools and methods to remove the cancerous growths and heal the wounds that plague America's democratic values and institutions.

In Part I some of the urban and rural facets of poverty are exposed. In August, 1966, the Senate Subcommittee on Executive Reorganization chaired by Senator Abraham Ribicoff (D.-Conn.) held a series of hearings on the "biggest domestic crisis ever," the eruptions of our cities that have reverberated from sea to shining sea. The main thrust of the hearings was to determine a strategy for easing the pressures and tensions in urban America and for instilling the principles of equality, freedom, and justice, which contrary to the American myth, have still not been extended to great masses of citizens.

Kenneth Clark poignantly recalls that the success of both the Manhattan Project and the Apollo Project was largely due to a firm national commitment and mandate that enabled the mobilization of manpower, funds and facilities to accomplish a finite goal in a relatively short period of time. These projects, once begun, gained momentum as they approached their objectives and were not continually pushed and pulled by shifting coalitions of political forces.

In a statement entitled, "The Services Strategy vs. The Income Strategy," Lee Rainwater underscores the theme that solving the poverty problem should precede tackling the question of urban management and in the process he offers a strong argument on one aspect of social priority setting.

Milton Kotler asserts that if local government is to be truly local, then the smallest unit of community vitality— the neighborhood—should be the basic building block upon which livable metropolitan areas should be constructed. He calls for establishing neighborhoods as tax-exempt corporations.

" 'There is Still Time ... But Not Much Time,' " cautions Herbert J. Gans, who sees segregation and poverty as the pivotal problems that underlie the sickness of our cities. These two are the first to be confronted; tangential palliatives can and should come later.

Daniel Moynihan points out that there is a great crisis in the cities but that few people realize it. In effect, they are largely unaware or would rather divert their attention to inspiring events such as the Apollo program. The lack of visibility of social problems is not unrelated to the second-class status which the social sciences have been given in government.

The rural-to-urban population shift which reached major proportions in the 50's and 60's but which has apparently tapered down in the recent past is indicative of the dynamics and interplay of urban and rural poverty in America. Urban problems are inextricably intertwined with rural problems. Rural migrants to the city, unaccustomed to the tempo of urban life, find it difficult, and often impossible, to develop a life style that enables them to cope with their new environment. But the problem does not stop there, as was so poignantly pointed out in the report, *The People Left Behind,* prepared by the President's Commission on Rural Poverty. While efforts to deal adequately with urban poverty are stifled by a lack of visibility of these problems in the American scene, rural poverty, even among social scientists, has just begun to take on the sense of urgency that it deserves.

In his article, "Life in Appalachia—the Case of Hugh McCaslin," Robert Coles provides a change of pace with a provocative portrayal of a single individual entrapped in the morass of rural poverty. It is reassuring to encounter a study which avoids broad generalities and concentrates on the individual as a human being rather than as a cipher. It is, after all, the fate of the Hugh McCaslins which hangs in the balance of the policy debate on the national anti-poverty program.

Problems will persist until adequate solutions are found, in the sense that the measures recommended and the programs proposed are brought to the attention of elected officials and other policy-makers. Part II of this book is devoted to two articles that suggest solutions to certain aspects of the all-encompassing problems of poverty and other conflicts derived therefrom.

Returning to the theme of visibility, Charlayne A. Hunter, in "On the Case In Resurrection City," opens her article by saying: "Resurrection City—where the poor had hoped to become visible and effective—is dead." But, she continues, it was: ". . . a moment in history that may yet have a telling effect on the future of this country." In other words, even failure can be fruitful if it is visible failure. The poor people's campaign illustrated how unorganized the poverty-stricken are and how difficult it is for such a group to compete with more highly organized lobby groups that can expertly defend their interests.

Finally, Martin Rein and S. M. Miller stress the need for a strategy to eliminate poverty in their article, "Poverty Programs and Policy Priorities."

Part III, the last section of the book, is devoted to mechanisms in the form of legislative proposals that have been designed to encourage the development of a strategy for the social sciences. The main argument is that problem identification and solution will not come rapidly and incisively unless federal, state and local institutions exist to provide the social sciences with the level and continuity of support together with the status and prestige that they deserve.

Senator Walter F. Mondale (D.-Minn.) argues in his "Report on the Social State of the Union" for the development of a stronger alliance between social scientists and policy-makers. He has introduced legislation that would create a Council of Social Advisors which would prepare a Social Report for the President's transmission to Congress. The Act would also create a Joint Congressional Committee on the Social Report. The bill was the subject of extensive hearings in 1967 when introduced as The Full Opportunity and Social Accounting Act, and again, in 1969 when reintroduced in the 91st Congress as the Full Opportunity Act.

In October, 1966, I first introduced the National Foundation for the Social Sciences Act (NSSF). Hearings that year and the subsequent year served to strengthen the case for enactment of the bill. In 1969 I reintroduced the bill, which is cosponsored by 32 Senators. Chances for passage in the Senate during the 91st Congress are favorable. The proposed NSSF would, as would The Full Opportunity Act, enhance the status of social scientists by virtue of a legislative mandate. The social sciences would receive a quantum leap in funding and acquire the support of Congress to conduct innovative and sometimes controversial research. It is the latter issue that has greatly hampered the growth of the social science program in the National Science Foundation. The Foundation had and still has, in spite of a recent reorganization act, a vague mandate for support of these important disciplines.

"The Case for—and Against—A National Social Science Foundation" contains an introductory sketch of the major elements of the bill and the primary issues that have been raised as of 1968. There follows a series of excerpts from the statements of government officials and noted social scientists who discuss the pros and cons of such an institutional innovation. (A slightly modified version of the bill that provides for the funding of research, education and training in the social sciences was introduced in 1969. Previously, only research was mentioned. The current proposed Foundation would no longer administer any research funds transferred from another agency. Another major change is that the Foundation would now be charged with the responsibility of preparing an annual report on the health and status of the social sciences.)

In summary, the three elements of a national strategy for the social sciences are: (1) highly visible social problems; (2) practical and comprehensive solutions; and (3) governmental mechanisms that serve to identify these problems and encourage the mobilization of funds, manpower and facilities for their solution.

Poverty is a national problem that has no geographical bias. It has haunted the conscience of America for at least a century. Nothing done today will automatically eradicate poverty tomorrow; but the momentum of the war on poverty must be sustained and our experimental temperament reinforced.

Poverty is urbanization and the resultant process of dehumanization. Poverty is the concrete jungle of the ghetto with a blade of grass here and there poking through a crack in a sidewalk. Poverty is also rural deterioration and decay and resultant dehumanization. It is rural sidewalks overgrown with weeds and grass.

The rural-to-urban population shift is, to borrow from the words of Karl Marx, a locomotive of history. However, this continuing influx of people to the cities, contrary to a Marxian deterministic concept of history, is the result of man-made policies and is not guided by an invisible hand as many "laissez-faire" demographers would contend.

The shift from farm and small town to city is no more inevitable than is poverty. They are both open to solutions.

What types of solutions can and should social scientists provide? First, a better understanding of human and social behavior is imperative, notwithstanding the challenges to conventional wisdom that are likely to result. Basic research should not be neglected, but should receive high priority. The root causes of social problems should be sought out, brought to the surface, and considered by policy-makers when designing new programs. These points have been made by the National Commission on Civil Disorders and the National Commission on the Causes and Prevention of Violence. Social scientists should help to design as well as evaluate programs. They should be policy-makers as well as work closely with policy-makers. Overall, there is a continuum from knowledge to power with active roles for social scientists to play along this entire spectrum.

Finally, there are new mechanisms needed, especially at the Federal level, that will enhance the chances of the social sciences to realize their potential and in the process relieve much of the pressure and strain on the American public. In addition, these sorely-needed institutions would encourage debate not only about the needs and uses of the social sciences but about the *politics* of the social sciences as well. Both components are prerequisites to devising a national strategy for these disciplines.

For such a debate The Full Opportunity Act provides forums—a Council of Social Advisors in the executive branch and a Joint Committee in the legislative branch, and a vehicle—the Social Report. Similarly, the NSSF would report yearly to the Congress on the status and health of the social sciences. These acts would serve to engender viable, stimulating, and continuous debate. Without public debate the social sciences cannot attain and retain significant visibility. And, without proper mechanisms, debate cannot occur. In this sense, the form of the dialogue is as important as the content.

This healthy exchange of ideas should help to increase the financial support for and the national visibility of the social sciences to a point where the eradication of some of the great social ills of our time can be accelerated. In this light a concerted effort to develop a national strategy for the social sciences deserves a very high place on our list of national priorities. It is imperative that intellectuals and policy-makers undertake this effort in a harmonious manner.

The United States Senate   *Fred R. Harris*
Washington, D. C.

Sick Cities...
And the Search for a Cure

INTRODUCTION. In August 1966, after three consecutive summers of urban riots, a Senate subcommittee headed by Abraham Ribicoff (D., Conn.) began inquiring into the role the Federal government should play in easing the problems of the cities—"our biggest domestic crisis ever," as Senator Ribicoff called it. The subcommittee invited about a hundred witnesses, from ghetto residents to big businessmen, to testify. The hearings ended 10 months later, in June, a few weeks before the ghettos of Newark, Detroit, and 70 other American cities erupted.

One major goal of the inquiry, Senator Ribicoff explained, was to help in devising a master plan for dealing with the cities. "Right now," he told *Trans-action,* "we have confusion, a lack of coordination, and programs at cross-purposes. We've passed program after program, all good and necessary programs, but we have no overall objective. We have a piecemeal approach. We need a systematic approach."

In conducting the inquiry, the subcommittee decided to call people in close touch with the problems of the cities, not people who, the Senators thought, saw these problems through a glass, distantly. (This was why the subcommittee saw fit to invite only two economists—though many of the proposals later suggested were economic proposals.) According to Senator Ribicoff, many urban experts had been talking only among themselves, taking in one another's brainwashing. Most of the social scientists invited, therefore, were to speak about what they knew from first-hand experience, from street-corner research. Extracts from the testimony of eight of these social scientists appear on the following pages.

All the social scientists agreed that the problems of the cities stem from racial injustice and poverty—or perhaps from poverty alone. The consensus was that the nation's current urban policies are bankrupt. A number of social scientists called for massive programs to create more jobs for the poor and the unskilled. Several argued for a guaranteed annual income—among them, political scientist Daniel Patrick Moynihan, who suggested family allowances, and sociologist Lee Rainwater, who spoke of his study of life at the Pruitt-Igoe public-housing project in St. Louis and urged that no one's income be permitted to fall below a certain point.

Psychologist Kenneth B. Clark supported the proposal for a guaranteed income, but with deep reservations. He suggested that an agency like the RAND Corporation be created to study urban problems. Sociologist Herbert J. Gans recommended a massive housing program and the creation of many more jobs. Milton Kotler, a political scientist, called for financial aid for neighborhood organizations working on behalf of ghetto residents. Economist Anthony Downs saw little benefit in the proposal for a guaranteed income, and called instead for the dispersal of the ghettos and for more new housing. George Sternlieb, a professor of business administration, endorsed an urban Homestead Act that would permit slum tenants to become property owners.

In short, while the social scientists were almost unanimous in their diagnosis, there was a good deal of disagreement about the best therapy.

Still, the testimony of the social scientists may have accomplished something. Senator Ribicoff went on to introduce a multi-measure "urban America" program, which called for (among other things) new cities to be created and for the government to become the "employer of the last resort." Also included: the establishment of a Congressional agency to evaluate past legislation, a suggestion of Professor Moynihan's. Senator Robert F. Kennedy (D., N.Y.), a subcommittee member, introduced bills to create jobs for slum residents and to construct new housing.

Senator Jacob K. Javits (R., N.Y.), another subcommittee member, even expressed limited support for a guaranteed income—a proposal endorsed by many of the social scientists. In an interview, Senator Javits said: "We may have to modify it, but the income maintenance proposal needs to be looked into urgently." Senator Ribicoff had shown interest in the idea early in the hearings, but apparently was swayed by the criticism he heard: "As Dr. Clark told us, the poor man needs to feel his individual worth. He needs wages, not handouts."

Perhaps the basic value of the hearings, though, lay in the very fact that they were held. They symbolized a mounting commitment on the part of certain not uninfluential Senators to solve the cities' problems. Looking back over the inquiry, for example, Senator Ribicoff maintained that action "is more urgent than ever. Nothing has changed.

It's only worse—this summer has proved that. But with this war in Asia, Congress is avoiding new programs costing money. Eventually Congress will have to face up to the explosive problems we exposed—and act to resolve them." Eventually? "Eventually," Senator Ribicoff emphasized, "is *today*."

THE URBAN NEGRO IS THE 'URBAN PROBLEM'

Daniel P. Moynihan

The central thesis of these hearings is that American society is facing an urban crisis. I seriously doubt that even a significant minority of the American people believe any such thing. The foundations of disbelief are varied but convergent. The principal one is that for a solid quarter century the great mass of Americans have experienced a steadily rising standard of living, in a measure without parallel in history. This rising level of well being has been accompanied by and in large measure has consisted of improvements in housing, transportation, education, health, recreation, and other "urban" amenities which are now said to be in a state of crisis, but which most persons know to be in a vastly better condition now than in times past. I believe it fair to say that this popular impression corresponds to whatever reality is reflected in our standard national statistics, and that a great many students of cities, however urgent they may feel is the need for further improvement, will nonetheless agree that things are far better now than they have ever been.

What then is the case for "crisis"? It rests largely, I believe, on three congeries of facts which are only somewhat related to each other, but which tend to be perceived with equal concern by persons interested in this sort of thing.

■ The first set of "facts" consists of assertions that American cities are ugly, incoherent, sprawling cultural wastelands. Los Angeles is the preferred example, and with good reason.

■ The second set of facts is addressed to the severe financial strains which most central cities are experiencing.

■ The third set concerns the growth of a large Negro lower class in those cities, a group that many seem to feel is less assimilable than lower class immigrant groups that have preceded it, and which recently has erupted in sporadic mass violence. . . . The appearance of large numbers of lower class Negroes in Northern cities has led many persons to assert that we are in the grip of a unique problem. It seems to me that it is not yet clear whether this is so, but it may turn out that it is. In the meantime I would certainly agree with James Q. Wilson that "for the present, the urban Negro is, in a fundamental sense, *the* 'urban problem.' "

But even here one is impressed with how easy it is for the great number of Americans to remain quite unaware of any such situation. The physical isolation of Negro housing is so near to complete in the United States that it is possible to live in the same city with a million Negro Americans and have only the faintest awareness that they live in distinct neighborhoods and communities that have vastly greater "urban" problems than those faced by the community at large. And such is the hold of race on the American mind that it becomes entirely too easy simply to assume that Negroes will act differently from whites, an assertion one hears increasingly from Negroes as well. I have often wondered, for example, what would be the reaction of the business community if it were reported that the "proletariat" were rioting in Los Angeles, or Cleveland, or Rochester, or wherever, instead of Negroes. Would there not be a deeper tremor of concern? It is a vicious but persisting fact of American life that white Americans accept as almost natural the fact that Negro Americans are mistreated and that in response they misbehave. And somehow whites contrive to dislike Negroes on both grounds.

In any event, it remains the case that only a limited number of Americans see contemporary problems as a result of the malfunctioning of that system of economic and social relationships that are defined as urban.

But there is yet another source of reluctance to accept the reality and urgency of urban problems which is more difficult to isolate—and impossible, I should think, to prove —that I would nonetheless presume to bring to your attention. I would call it the "crisis in confidence" with regard to the efforts that have already been made to deal with the urban problem.

. . . The American public supports a fantastic array of social services, and does so in ever larger amounts. The issue, then, is not whether, but which. Thus, with regard to persons living in or near to poverty, a fundamental issue is to choose between a strategy of services, which Shriver's proposal would entail, as against a strategy of income. The amounts of money a Project Keep Moving would require are in the range of those that would be needed to establish a national family allowance. I can imagine a good argument being made that if there is an extra thousand dollars a year to go round for every family in the nation, or every poor family, that the best thing would be to give them the cash and let them spend it on things they think they need most—which might well be formal education for many, but would surely be more varied than any formula laid down in Washington would permit. In any event, to propose spending the money on services, which such research as we have suggests will produce little or no effect, is to risk being thought ridiculous or worse by members of the public, and we would delude ourselves if we did not see that this judgment has already been reached by large numbers. . . .

I believe our difficulty here has two quite different components. The first is that our commitment to evaluation research is, as Peter Rossi states, fundamentally ambivalent; one of attraction and fear, trust and distrust. This is so not only because research of this kind can blow up in an administrator's face when it turns out his programs show little or none of the effects they are supposed to achieve, but more importantly, because in areas of social policy, facts are simply not neutral, however much we would hope to treat them as such. In social science, data are political. Most social arrangements rest on assumptions about the "facts" of a given situation. To challenge such facts is also to challenge those social arrangements, as Louis Wirth has observed. As distinguished a social scientist as Walter B. Miller has suggested that because this is so there may even be "a direct incompatibility between careful evaluative research and the political process." Certainly we would agree that research findings, which are almost invariably complex, cautious, and qualified, and often indicate the most modest impacts, are hardly attuned to political rhetoric.

The second source of difficulty, however, is of quite a different nature. It is that up until now the executive branch of the federal government, and the executive branch in American government in general, has had a virtual monopoly on the product of evaluation research. Congress, the state legislatures, the city councils, are simply told what have been the results of such research. They do not have to agree, but they are hard put to disagree.

There is nothing sinister about this state of affairs. Serious evaluation research, as I have said, is only just reaching the state of a developed—as against an experimental—technique. Inevitably it has been sponsored in the first instance by executive departments. However, because the findings of such research are not neutral, it would be almost dangerous to permit this imbalance to persist. There are a number of reasons. First, and most important, the Congress and other legislative bodies are put at a considerable disadvantage. A major weapon in the "arsenal of persuasion" is in effect denied them. Second, the executive is exposed to the constant temptation to release only those findings that suit its purposes; there is no one to keep them honest. Third, universities and other private groups which often undertake such research on contract are in some measure subject to constant if subtle pressure to produce "positive" findings. The simple fact is that a new source of knowledge is coming into being; while it is as yet an imperfect technique, it is likely to improve, and if it comes to be accepted as a standard element in public discourse it is likely to raise considerably the level of that discourse. This source of knowledge should not remain an executive monopoly.

How is Congress to respond? I would offer a simple analogy. In the time this nation was founded, the principal form in which knowledge was recorded and preserved was in printed books, and accordingly in 1800 Congress established the Library. Over the next century, techniques of accounting and budgeting developed very rapidly, and in 1921 Congress established the General Accounting Office. I would like to suggest that Congress might now establish an Office of Legislative Evaluation which would have the task of systematically evaluating the results of the social and economic programs enacted by it and paid for out of public monies. Such an office could be established as a separate agency, or it could be located in the Library of Congress or the General Accounting Office. But the essential feature must be that it will be staffed by professional social scientists who will routinely assess the results of government programs in the same manner that the GAO routinely audits them. It should not be expected that their findings will be dramatic or quick in coming, or that they will put an end to argument—just the contrary is likely to occur. But the long-run effect could be immensely useful. The Congress could develop in its terms a series of data comparable to the social indicators which the executive branch is now developing. I would like to make clear also that such an office should concern itself as much with matters such as the farm program or the merchant marine program as with those concerned with poverty or health or education.

THE INTERESTS OF THE PRIVILEGED ARE AT STAKE

Kenneth B. Clark

The first approach to dealing with problems of slums, which became the basis of our social welfare system, is by trying to help these people in "Lady Bountiful" style— charity, community centers, or things of that sort. It is clear that this did not work—with increased social services, we got increased pathology. The predicament of people in the slums did not improve as a result of social services; the only thing that happened was that the social agencies and social services became more affluent.

The antipoverty program is another attempt to deal with the problems of the slums, and it seems to be based on a new approach. Unlike the older social service approach which tried to do things for people or give charity to people, the core of the antipoverty program, when I was involved in trying to develop this rationale, was that people should be helped to help themselves. Community action was considered the key new approach to rehabilitating people in the slums.

I think two or three years of evidence would lead to a candid assessment that this has not worked any better than the old social service approach. The emphasis on community action for effective solution of slum problems seems to be more verbal than actual. Wherever we found any attempt at significant community action as part of the antipoverty programs, almost invariably political considerations intervened to truncate or control or restrict the extent of community action which local political figures would permit. . . .

When our society is serious about solving any given social, economic, or military problem, it mobilizes the best brains and experts in the particular field and provides them with the financial resources, the facilities, and the power necessary to understand and to solve that basic problem. This was certainly the approach which we used in developing the atomic and nuclear bombs, and it was the approach which we used in achieving our successes in exploration of outer space. This was the basis upon which the Air Force set up the RAND Corporation 20 years ago. . . .

I think the budget is about as good an index of the priority society gives various problems as one can find. Our space program and our Vietnam war have budgetary supports which indicate tremendous seriousness. Our antipoverty programs have budgetary indications of secondary, tertiary, peripheral priorities, and I don't think that we will solve the problems of our inner cities by relegating them to peripheral priorities. If we are really serious about solving the problems of our ghettos and reversing the pathology and plight of our cities, we must use the same approach we use in these other areas.

I am proposing—and am now involved in trying to set up—at least the nucleus of a RAND Corporation type of center for the study and solution of urban ghetto problems. This center in its initial form is an independently funded consortium in the fields of social science, municipal and public affairs, consumer interests. Experts will be brought together to monitor all areas of governmental services and programs to assure that the rights of the poor, the victims of our slums and ghettos, and the underprivileged in our cities are not ignored; that these people are no longer short-changed as they have callously been in the past; that their share in the economic and political benefits of the society will not be lost or preempted by others; and that their civil, legal, and constitutional rights are not ignored or disregarded because of their lack of power to protect themselves. It is my hope that these specialists would function on behalf of the poor in ways similar to the ways in which more privileged middle class individuals and groups function for themselves. I am trying to determine whether it is possible to systematize and organize empathy. The primary and exclusive goal of these experts would be the representation and assistance of the poor—not representation in the literal sense of being elected by them, but of being concerned with their welfare as if it were our own that was at stake (and, by the way, I don't think this is an abstract point).

I think that we are going to become serious about the problems of our cities and our slums and our ghettos only when more privileged people understand that the pathology of the ghettos cannot be confined to the ghettos and that the interests of the privileged are at stake. There is no immunity to the consequences of squalor.

THE SERVICES STRATEGY VS. THE INCOME STRATEGY

Lee Rainwater

There seem to me to be two different kinds of urban problems, although each deeply affects the other. Efforts to solve the general problems of *urban management* will forever be frustrated—or at least much, much more costly—without a solution to the *problem of poverty,* both urban and rural. Unless the poverty problem is solved, every urban service will have to be seriously distorted and fragmented in order either to avoid or to take special account of the problems posed by having an "other America." For this reason, as well as for reasons of simple human justice, first priority in dealing with urbanization as our major domestic problem should be given to the elimination of poverty.

The elimination of poverty has a very simple referent. It means that the present income distribution in the nation —in which a small group of the population earns a great deal of money, a large proportion earns a more moderate amount of income, and a small proportion earns very little —must be changed by moving that bottom portion up into the middle category. In short, the current diamond-shaped income distribution must be changed into one which has the shape of a pyramid. I'm speaking here about family income rather than individual income.

There is certainly nothing wrong with a teenage boy earning $1.50 an hour while he goes to school or while he learns a trade. But there is something very wrong about that kind of income for a head of a family with two or three children, or for a man who would like to be the head of a family but cannot afford to be.

This redistribution would channel national income, particularly the yearly increment in national income, to families in the lower 30 to 40 percent of the population, so that a family income floor is established which is not too far below the median income for American families as a whole. If we can accomplish this, we will have succeeded in creating an urban society in which, while problems may still be difficult, they will not seem nearly so insoluble, because we will not have to plan for two kinds of Americans, the average American and the deprived American, as we do now.

It seems to me that there are basically two strategies implicit in the various programs and suggested plans for doing something about poverty: One, by far the most entrenched at present, might be called the *services strategy*, and the other, the *income strategy*.

The services strategy involves the design of special services for the poor. The problem with the services approach is that to a considerable extent it carries the latent assumption that either the poor are permanently poor and, therefore, must have special services, or that the poor can be changed while they are still poor, and that once they have changed, they will then be able to [function] in ways that will do away with their poverty. I think these assumptions are extremely pernicious ones.

One problem with the services approach is that the priority of needs of the poor is categorically established when the service programs are set up and funded. For example, the federal public housing program provides a service to each household in Pruitt-Igoe in the form of a subsidized apartment that costs about $545 a year—that is the subsidy. This subsidy amounts to a fifth of the mean family income of the tenants in the project. It is very likely that from the point of view of the needs of many of the families who live in Pruitt-Igoe that $545 could be put to much better use.

For another example, the Council of the White House Conference "To Fulfill These Rights" recommended that one program to help do away with Negro disadvantage could be to increase the average school expenditure per child $500 per year. Consider a poor family with three or four school children. Such an increase would mean devoting $1,500 to $2,000 a year to better educational facilities for that family's children. Yet, might it not be that, because of its effect on the family environment, an increase of $1,500 to $2,000 in that family's income would have as much or more educational effect on those children than would a comparable expenditure of resources in the school?

Finally, special programs for the poor are extremely difficult to design so that they do not have the effect of furthering the stigmatized status of the poor. To design services which do not stigmatize at the same time that they try to serve seems to pose tremendous political, administrative, and human engineering tasks, for which past experience gives us little reason to believe we have the skills.

Most of those who have studied the actual operation of service programs catering to an exclusively lower class clientele have been impressed by the demeaning and derogation of the poor that goes along with the service. The principal power that the poor want is the power of money in their pockets to make these choices as they see fit and as the needs of their families dictate.

The second poverty elimination strategy, the income strategy, goes a long way toward avoiding the difficulties that past experience suggests are inherent in the services strategy. Here the task is to develop a set of economic programs that have the direct result of providing poor families and individuals with an adequate income. There are good reasons from the social science information now available to us for believing that the most powerful and immediate resource to assist the poor to cope with their problems, not only the problems of economic disadvantage, but all of the dependent problems of community pathology, individual lack of motivation, and the like—the most powerful resource is income.

We know, for example, that when a man has a job and an adequate income, he is more respected in his home, and he is less likely to desert or divorce his wife. If one wishes to reverse those effects of lower class adaptations that are unconstructive, the most direct way of doing it is to strike at the root of the problem—at the lack of an income sufficient to live out a stable "good American life" style.

Having said this, I leave the field of sociological expertise because the problems are then ones that require the technical competence of an economist. Those economists who have pursued this line of thinking in studying the problem of poverty have suggested that an income strategy requires three elements:

■ An aggregational approach—that is, tight full employment—with a low, a very low, real unemployment rate—that is, an unemployment rate that takes into account labor force dropouts.

■ Second, a structural approach, which compensates the tendency for unemployment among low skilled workers to remain at high levels even when over-all unemployment is low. Such an approach would require that federal programs to bring about full employment be tied to guarantees of labor force entry jobs for unskilled men, and guarantees of training on the job to upgrade those skills. In this context, a high minimum wage would also be necessary and would not have the negative effect of hastening the replacement of men by machines.

■ Finally, an income maintenance program, which fills in

the income gap not touched by the tight full employment programs. The income maintenance program would be required for families with a disabled or no male head, and where the wife should not work because of the ages or numbers of the children.

Such a program could take the form of family allowances or a negative income tax or an annual guaranteed income, but in any case should involve a major reorganization of the government's current income maintenance programs, notably ADC and other types of public assistance, since these current programs are by far the most stigmatizing poverty programs now in existence.

If the first two employment strategies were as successful as some economists feel they might be, the dollar investment in an income maintenance program could be quite small. However, such a program would have considerable long-run importance, since it would serve as proof of a more permanent national commitment to a more equal income distribution, and as a yearly goal to the federal government to plan the economy in such a way that no more than a very small number of families are without an adequate bread-winner. . . .

MAKING LOCAL GOVERNMENT TRULY LOCAL

Milton Kotler

. . . The facts of urban poverty are these: Unemployment is rotten, education is poor, health is bad. Together, these factors impose a menacing condition. Yet there is encouragement in this committee's deliberation, and indeed in recent legislative moves. It represents a commitment within the government to apply some of its wealth and know-how to this urban crisis.

Now the choice is between the existing despair and the new hope. How is the task to be done? What is the proper method of action to rebuild the slum? What is the proper role of different agents of change—public and private, federal, state, and local—to assist this measure? I think the crucial question is whether we find the method. The country has wealth, but we are often short on concept. The real test is to find the concept of change and apply our resources to it.

To my mind, that concept is neighborhood self-governing decision. The neighborhood, constituted as a non-profit, tax-exempt, democratically structured corporation with its own assembly, officials, and revenues, is the principal agent of change to rebuild our slums into a legal community of culture, freedom, and prosperity. The neighborhood must become a legal community of self-help and self-governing decisions with sufficient capacity to relate to other organizations, public and private, for the resources and assistance to build a better city.

There is a lot of talk today about the neighborhoods being gone, not very viable in the new technological age. I grant the scepticism, but I also want to introduce the fact that the neighborhood is a living reality in the lives of people who live in our cities. The neighborhood is the last remaining unit, territorial unit, of public confidence in our cities.

There is often little confidence in the city government. The neighborhood is the last unit of public confidence, and therefore, one must apply to that unit of public confidence the instrumentalities of legal self-governing decision and resources to act on this problem.

The neighborhood must be strengthened by organization and legal incorporation. It must be legitimized by democratic structure and public authority over resources to decide and act on specific local matters of the neighborhood. It might be 7,000 people or indeed in our densest, largest cities it is quite conceivable to view neighborhoods as groups of 100,000 or more.

The neighborhood as a legal community must become the principal agent in rebuilding its locality and governing the public matters that intimately affect the lives of its residents. Further, neighborhood corporations must be responsible to each and every resident through democratic structure, and also responsible, through their legal agency and powers, to outside authorities, public and private.

Our cities are too large. Today New York is the size our nation was when it was first constituted. Today many cities are larger than states were in an earlier day. . . .

Today, the field of humanity and popular hope in the slums is the territory of their neighborhood community. The expression of hope is through neighborhood decision. Structure that hope into the neighborhood corporation, and let that hope exercise itself legally and practically upon the material conditions of poverty. If the impoverished conditions of slum life are political, and indeed all the poor conditions constitute a political condition of oppression, the method of change is simply political independence and freedom, which incorporates the neighborhood for decision, and uses the resources of technology and the wealth of a nation to do the task.

■ The neighborhood area must be organized as a tax-exempt corporation based on one man-one vote assembly and membership.

■ It must be territorially bound.

■ It must be democratically structured on the basis of assembly, officials, and funding.

■ It must be formed to govern something public.

The neighborhood corporations must have authority to

govern certain matters of social service or economic development that intimately affect their local life. The neighborhood corporation must relate, in its practice of decision and of management of services, to all appropriate public and private agencies and organizations. It must be a part of the way of performing public services in the city.

This argument is practical as it reflects two years of experience in Columbus [Ohio] in the ECCO project. ECCO (the East Central Citizens Organization) is today a tax-exempt neighborhood corporation of 7,000 residents in a poor area of the city. Its territory is one square mile. Its population is 70 percent Negro and 30 percent white. Unemployment is high. The median income is about $3,000. Housing is substandard. And in many respects it corresponds to poverty areas elsewhere.

Today, however, ECCO is no longer a desperate slum, because of its corporation and the action and decision of its citizens in assembly, council, and administration, in deciding the affairs of that community. ECCO is not just a poor community, but a poor community building its prosperity through dignity and independence. For the first time in the lives of its residents, that neighborhood community is an integral part of the life of the city. . . .

ECCO has the support of its people and the city. There are no riots in ECCO because ECCO has the authority to decide and govern affairs. Politicians do speak to ECCO in assembly and council. There is communication between the people of ECCO and the city, because ECCO is itself a government and has representative elective officials. . . .

This experience, I think, evidences the need for this new unit, the neighborhood corporation. I would suggest that the federal government currently fund the governing structures of neighborhood corporations around the country. . . . Direct funding can be used in many cities to set up the governing structure of neighborhood corporations, which in our case runs about $150,000.

Once formed, the neighborhood corporations can move toward delegate agencies to local community action organizations for program funding. But also under other legislation for housing grants, education grants, and so forth. In that connection I would sincerely urge a legislative thrust at amending such legislation in housing, labor, and other departments to develop the ability for the federal government to grant directly to neighborhood corporations as non-profit agencies. . . .

"THERE IS STILL TIME . . . BUT NOT MUCH TIME"

Herbert J. Gans

On the basis of 15 years of research and practice as a sociologist and city planner, I am convinced that the major problems of the city have almost nothing to do with the city. Instead, they can all be traced, directly and indirectly, to two sources, the *poverty* and the *segregation* faced by an increasing number of city dwellers. Poverty and segregation are the basic causes of slums, for when people cannot afford decent housing and are discriminated against, they *must* overcrowd the oldest and least desirable buildings of the city. The despair that results from poverty and segregation encourages such desperate acts as delinquency, addiction, and family and personal breakdown, as well as ghetto unrest and rioting. These acts help to encourage the white middle class exodus to the suburbs, and this in turn deprives cities of municipal revenues, and downtown retail districts of profitable customers, which hasten their decline. And the fear of poor and nonwhite city voters nurtures the suburban opposition to metropolitan solutions, as well as the backlash voting patterns of blue and white collar urban residents whom I call the not-so-affluent.

The urban crisis is also rural, for the cities attract, as they always have, people who seek relief from worse poverty and segregation in rural areas. The crisis is thus national; it has to do with economic and social inequality in the nation as a whole. That crisis is above all economic, for it is *poverty* that causes social and individual breakdown, and it is the *poverty* and *poverty-induced behavior* of the slum dwellers, not their race, which brings on the fears that drive affluent whites to the suburbs and not-so-affluent ones to violent opposition against open housing. And urban poverty is in turn largely the result of *unemployment* and *perhaps even more of underemployment;* of being limited to underpaid, insecure, dirty, dead-end jobs.

Consequently, the best—and probably the only—solution for America's urban problems is to enable the poor, the unemployed, and the underemployed to obtain the jobs and incomes that will incorporate them into the affluent society. Once this is accomplished, the remaining problems of the city can be solved more easily, and the class-based opposition to racial integration will disapppear. . . .

The experience of urban renewal and public housing suggests that neither program has helped the poor significantly. In too many cities, where inexpensive housing was already in short supply, the clearing and rehabilitation of slums only forced poor people to pay yet higher rents, often in other slums. Incidentally, urban renewal did not even achieve its aim of luring middle class people back to the city. And moving poor people into public housing did not solve their basic problems. It is clear that just giving poor people better housing cannot eliminate their poverty.

We must therefore turn our approach upside down: to eliminate the poverty of the poor so that they can afford decent housing and solve their other problems as well. Consequently, the prime goal of any housing program must be to create jobs for the unemployed and underemployed even while it creates good housing for them and renews the cities.

Such a housing program should consist of three elements. First, it should encourage the building of millions of new federally subsidized "moderate" and "middle" income, racially integrated units in cities, suburbs, and new towns, much like the units already being built with the help of FHA's nonprofit housing program, and other federal and state subsidies. Second, rent supplements should be provided on a much larger scale to enable poor people to choose new or older units, and third, the dwellings and neighborhoods of the slums must be rebuilt and rehabilitated.

This housing program should create as many new jobs as possible. Moreover, it would enable the recipients of these jobs to choose new or old housing like all other Americans, and [even more] to do so with rent supplements. It would also press forward on urban and suburban integration at the same time as the ghettos are rebuilt for those who prefer to remain in familiar neighborhoods. I suspect that if nonwhite people had free choice in housing, many would remain in their present neighborhoods, and only a small number would now choose the suburbs. Consequently, the suburban fear of inundation by former slum-dwellers is groundless. I suspect that this is the case, but because of the lack of housing and other urban research, we do not really know, just as we do not know much about the real effects of urban renewal, or about what people—poor, affluent, and not-so-affluent—want and need in their communities. . . .

New income and job-creating programs will be costly, but A. Philip Randolph's Freedom Budget suggests that the

funds can come just from the increases in national productivity in the next decade. They will also be controversial,
but if they are not carried out, we can expect a steady rise
in the self-destructive and anti-social behavior of the city's
poor, as well as in demonstrations and riots, especially if
other Americans continue to become more affluent. . . . Increased pathology and violence are not only social dangers
per se, but they will surely be met by public demands for
repressive actions and for retrenchment in governmental
anti-poverty efforts, and repression and retrenchment can
only result in yet more pathology and violence in return.
This would create a vicious circle of pathology, repression,
more pathology, more repression, that could spiral into
really widespread pathological behavior and open class
warfare in the years to come. Then the taste of affluence
will be bitter, and the American way of life not worth living even for the affluent. . . .

October 1967

Life in Appalachia...
The Case of Hugh McCaslin

ROBERT COLES

Hugh McCaslin is unforgettable. He has red hair and, at 43, freckles. He stands six feet four. As he talked to me about his work in the coal mines, I kept wondering what he did with his height down inside the earth.

Once he must have been an unusually powerful man; even today his arms and legs are solid muscle. The fat he has added in recent years has collected in only one place, his waist, both front and back.

"I need some padding around my back; it's hurt, and I don't think it'll ever get back right. I broke it bad working, and they told me at first they'd have it fixed in no time flat, but they were wrong. I don't know if they were fooling themselves, or out to fool me in the bargain. It's hard to know *what's* going on around here—that's what I've discovered these last few years.

"I'll tell you, a man like me, he has a lot of time to think.

He'll sit around here, day upon day, and what else does
he have to keep his mind on but his thoughts? I can't
work, and even if I could, there's no work to do, not
around here, no sir. They told me I'm 'totally incapaci-
tated,' that's the words they used. They said my spine was
hurt, and the nerves, and I can't walk and move about
the way I should. As if I needed them to tell me!

"Then they gave me exercises and all, and told me I
was lucky, because even though I wasn't in shape to go
in the mines, I could do anything else, anything that's
not too heavy. Sometimes I wonder what goes on in the
heads of those doctors. They look you right in the eye,
and they're wearing a straight face on, and they tell you
you're sick, you've been hurt digging out coal, and you'll
never be the same, but you're really not so bad off, because
your back isn't so bad you can't be a judge, or a professor,
or the president of the coal company or something like
that, you know."

Once Hugh McCaslin (not his real name) asked
me to look at an X-ray taken of his back and his
shoulders—his vertebral column. He persuaded the
company doctor to give him the X-ray, or so he said.
(His wife told me that he had, in fact, persuaded
the doctor's secretary to hand it over, and tell her
boss—if he ever asked—that somehow the patient's
"file" had been lost.) He was convinced that the
doctor was a "company doctor"—which he assuredly
was—and a "rotten, dishonest one." Anyway, what
did I see in that X-ray? I told him that I saw very
little. I am no radiologist, and whatever it was that
ailed him could not be dramatically pointed out on
an X-ray, or if it could I was not the man to do it.
Well, yes he did know that, as a matter of fact:

"I got my nerves smashed down there in an accident.

I don't know about the bones. I think there was a lot of pressure, huge pressure on the nerves, and it affected the way I walk. The doctor said it wasn't a fracture on a big bone, just one near the spine. He said it wasn't 'too serious,' that I'd be O.K., just not able to go back to work, at least down there.

"Then, you see, they closed down the mine itself. That shows you I wasn't very lucky. My friends kept telling me I was lucky to be alive, and lucky to be through with it, being a miner. You know, we don't scare very easy. Together, we never would talk about getting hurt. I suppose it was somewhere in us, the worry; but the first time I heard my friends say anything like that was to me, not to themselves. They'd come by here when I was sick, and they'd tell me I sure was a fortunate guy, and God was smiling that day, and now He'd be smiling forever on me, because I was spared a *real* disaster, and it was bound to come, one day or another. It kind of got me feeling funny, hearing them talk like that *around my bed,* and then seeing them walk off real fast, with nothing to make *them* watch their step and take a pain pill every few hours.

"But after a while I thought maybe they did have something; and if I could just recover me a good pension from the company, and get my medical expenses all covered—well, then, I'd get better, as much as possible, and go fetch me a real honest-to-goodness job, where I could see the sun all day, and the sky outside, and breathe our air here, as much of it as I pleased, without a worry in the world.

"But that wasn't to be. I was dumb, real dumb, and hopeful. I saw them treating me in the hospital, and when they told me to go home I thought I was better, or soon would be. Instead, I had to get all kinds of treatments, and they said I'd have to pay for them, out of my savings or somewhere. And the pension I thought I was supposed to get, that was all in my mind, they said. They said the coal industry was going through a lot of changes, and you couldn't expect them to keep people going indefinitely, even if they weren't in the best of shape, even if it did happen down in the mines.

"Well, that's it, to make it short. I can't do hard work, and I have a lot of pain, every day of my life. I might be able to do light work, desk work, but hell, I'm not fit for anything like that; and even if I could, where's the work to be found? Around here? Never in a million years. We're doomed here, to sitting and growing the food we can and sharing our misery with one another.

"My brother, he helps; and my four sisters, they help; and my daddy, he's still alive and he can't help except to sympathize, and tell me it's a good thing I didn't get killed in that landslide and can see my boys grow up. He'll come over here and we start drinking. You bet, he's near 80, and we start drinking, and remembering. My daddy will ask me if I can recollect the time I said I'd save a thousand dollars for myself by getting a job in the mines and I say I sure can, and can he recollect the time he said I'd better not get too greedy, because there's bad that comes with good in this world, and especially way down there inside the earth."

He will take a beer or two and then get increasingly angry. His hair seems to look wilder, perhaps because he puts his hands through it as he talks. His wife becomes nervous and tries to give him some bread or crackers, and he becomes sullen or embarrassingly direct with her. She is trying to "soak up" his beer. She won't even let it hit his stomach and stay there a while. She wants it back. He tells her, "Why don't you *keep* your beer, if you won't let it do a thing for me?"

They have five sons, all born within nine years. The oldest is in high school and dreams of the day he will join the army. He says he will be "taken" in, say, in Charleston or Beckley—in his mind, any "big city" will do. He will be sent off to California or Florida or "maybe New York" for basic training; eventually he will "land himself an assignment— anywhere that's good, and it'll be far away from here, I do believe that." Hugh McCaslin becomes enraged when he hears his son talk like that; with a few beers in him he becomes especially enraged:

"That's the way it is around here. That's what's hap- pened to us. That's what they did to us. They made us lose any honor we had. They turned us idle. They turned us into a lot of grazing sheep, lucky to find a bit of pasture here and there. We don't *do* anything here any- more; and so my boys, they'll all want to leave, and they will. But they'll want to come back, too—because this land, it's in their bones going way back, and you don't shake off your ancestors that easy, no sir.

"My daddy, he was born right up the road in this here hollow, and his daddy, and back to a long time ago. There isn't anyone around here we're not kin to somehow, near or far. My daddy was the one supposed to leave for the mines. He figured he could make more money than he could dream about, and it wasn't too far to go. He went for a while, but some years later he quit. He couldn't take it. I grew up in a camp near the mine, and I'd still be there if it wasn't that I got hurt and moved back here to the hollow. Even while we were at the camp we used to come back here on Sundays, I remember, just like now they come here on weekends from Cincinnati and Dayton and those places, and even from way off in Chicago. I can recall the car we got; everybody talked about it, and when we'd drive as near here as we could—well, the people would come, my grandparents and all my uncles and aunts and cousins, and they'd look and look at that Ford, before they'd see if it was *us,* and say hello to us. I can recollect in my mind being shamed and wanting to disappear in one of those pockets, where my daddy would keep his pipes. My mother would say it wasn't they didn't want to see us, but the Ford, it was real special to them, and could you blame them for not looking at us?

"That was when things were really good. Except that even then I don't think we were all that contented. My mother always worried. Every day, come 3 or so in the afternoon, I could tell she was starting to worry. Will anything happen? Will he get hurt? Will they be coming over soon, to give me some bad news? (No, we had no telephone, and neither did the neighbors.) It got so we'd come home from school around 2 or so, and just sit there with her, pretending—pretending to do things, and say things. And then he'd come in, every time. We could hear his voice coming, or his steps, or the door, and we'd all loosen up—and pretend again, that there was nothing we'd worry about, because there wasn't nothing *to* worry about.

"One day—I think I was seven or eight, because I was in school, I know that—we had a bad scare. Someone came to the school and told the teacher something, whispered it in her ear. She turned into a sheet, and she looked as though she'd start crying. The older kids knew what had happened, just from her looks. (Yes, it was a one-room schoolhouse, just like the one we have here, only a little bigger.) They ran out, and she almost took off after them, except for the fact that she remembered us. So she turned around and told us there that something bad had happened down in the mines, an explosion, and we should go home and wait there, and if our mothers weren't there—well, wait until they got home.

"But we wanted to go with her. Looking back at it, I think she worried us. So she decided to take us, the little ones. And I'll tell you, I can remember that walk with her like it was just today. I can see it, and I can tell you what she said, and what we did, and all. We walked and walked, and then we came through the woods and there they were, all of a sudden before our eyes. The people there, just standing around and almost nothing being said between them. It was so silent I thought they'd all turn around and see us, making noise. But, you see, we must have stopped talking, too, because for a while they didn't even give us a look over their shoulders. Then we come closer, and I could hear there was noise after all: The women were crying, and there'd be a cough or something from some of the miners.

"That's what sticks with you, the miners wondering if their buddies were dead or alive down there. Suddenly I saw my father, and my mother. They were with their arms about one another—real unusual—and they were waiting, like the rest.

"Oh, we got home that night, yes, and my daddy said they were gone—they were dead and we were going away. And we did. The next week we drove here in our Ford, and I can hear my daddy saying it wasn't worth it, money and a car, if you die young, or you live but your lungs get poisoned, and all that, and you never see the sun except on Sundays.

"But what choice did he have? And what choice did I have? I thought I might want to do some farming, like my grandfather, but there's no need for me, and my grandfather couldn't really keep more than himself going, I mean with some food and all. Then I thought it'd be nice to finish school, and maybe get a job someplace near, in a town not a big city. But everything was collapsing all over the country then, and you'd be crazy to think you were going to get anything by leaving here and going out there, with the lines standing for soup—oh yes, we heard on the radio what it was like all over.

"It could be worse, you say to yourself, and you resolve to follow your daddy and be a miner. That's what I did. He said we had a lousy day's work, but we got good pay, and we could buy things. My daddy had been the richest man in his family for a while. In fact, he was the only man in his family who had any money at all. After the family looked over our Ford, they'd give us that real tired and sorry look, as though they needed some help real bad, and that's when my daddy would hand out the dollar bills, one after the other. I can picture it right now. You feel rich, and you feel real kind."

Hugh McCaslin's life wouldn't be that much better even if he had not been seriously hurt in a mine accident. The miners who were his closest friends are now unemployed, almost every one of them. They do not feel cheated out of a disability pension, but for all practical purposes he and they are equally idle, equally bitter, equally sad. With no prompting from my psychiatric mind he once put it this way:

"They talk about depressions in this country. I used to hear my daddy talk about them all the time, depressions. It wasn't so bad for my daddy and me in the thirties, when the Big One, the Big Depression, was knocking everyone down, left and right. He had a job, and I knew I was going to have one as soon as I was ready, and I did. Then when the war come, they even kept me home. They said we were keeping everything going over here in West Virginia. You can't run factories without coal. I felt I wouldn't mind going, and getting a look at things out there, but I was just as glad to stay here, I guess. I was married, and we were starting with the kids, so it would have been hard. My young brother, he went. He wasn't yet a miner, and they just took him when he was 18, I think. He come back here and decided to stay out of the mines, but it didn't make much difference in the end, anyway. We're all out of the mines now around here.

"So, you see it's *now* that *we're* in a depression. They say things are pretty good in most parts of the country, from what you see on TV, but not so here. We're in the biggest depression ever here: We have no money, and no welfare payments, and we're expected to scrape by like dogs. It gets to your mind after a while. You feel as low as can be, and nervous about everything. That's what a depression does, makes you dead broke, with a lot of bills and the lowest spirits you can ever picture a man having. Sometimes I get up and I'm ready to go over to an undertaker and tell him to do something with me real fast."

I have spent days and nights with the McCaslin family, and Hugh McCaslin doesn't always feel that "low," that depressed, that finished with life. I suppose it can be said that he has "adapted" to the hard, miserable life he faces. At times he shouts and screams about "things," and perhaps in that way keeps himself explicitly angry rather than sullen and brooding. His friends call him a "firebrand," and blame his temper on his red hair. In fact, he says what they are thinking, and need to hear said by someone. They come to see him, and in Mrs. McCaslin's words, "get him going." They bring him home-made liquor to help matters along.

The McCaslins are early risers, but no one gets up earlier than the father. He suffers pain at night; his back and his legs hurt. He has been told that a new hard mattress would help, and hot baths, and aspirin. He spends a good part of the night awake —"thinking and dozing off and then coming to, real sudden-like, with a pain here or there." For a while he thought of sleeping on the floor, or trying to get another bed, but he could not bear the prospect of being alone:

"My wife, Margaret, has kept me alive. She has some

of God's patience in her, that's the only way I figure she's
been able to last it. She smiles when things are so dark
you'd think the end has come. She soothes me, and tells
me it'll get better, and even though I know it won't I
believe her for a few minutes, and that helps."

So he tosses and turns in their bed, and his wife
has learned to sleep soundly but to wake up prompt-
ly when her husband is in real pain. They have aspirin and treat it as something special—and expensive. I think Hugh McCaslin realizes that he suffers
from many different kinds of pain; perhaps if he
had more money he might have been addicted to all
sorts of pain-killers long ago. Certainly when I
worked in a hospital I saw patients like him—hurt
and in pain, but not "sick" enough to require hospitalization, and in fact "chronically semi-invalids."
On the other hand, such patients had tried and failed
at any number of jobs. We will never know how
Hugh McCaslin might have felt today if he had
found suitable work after his accident, or had received further medical care. Work is something a
patient needs as he starts getting better, as anyone
who works in a "rehabilitation unit" of a hospital
well knows. Hugh McCaslin lacked medical care
when he needed it, lacks it today, and in his own
words needs a "time-killer" as much as a pain-killer.
His friends despair, drink, "loaf about," pick up
a thing here and there to do, and "waste time real
efficiently." So does he—among other things, by
dwelling on his injured body.

He dwells on his children, too. There are five of
them, and he wants all of them to leave West Vir-

ginia. Sometimes in the early morning, before his wife is up, he leaves bed to look at them sleeping:

"I need some hope, and they have it, in their young age and the future they have, if they only get the hell out of here before it's too late. Oh, I like it here, too. It's pretty, and all that. It's peaceful. I'm proud of us people. We've been here a long time, and we needed real guts to stay and last. And who wants to live in a big city? I've been in some of our cities, here in West Virginia, and they're no big value, from what I can see, not so far as bringing up a family. You have no land, no privacy, a lot of noise, and all that. But if it's between living and dying, I'll take living; and right here, right now, I think we're dying—dying away, slow but sure, every year more and more so."

He worries about his children in front of them. When they get up they see him sitting and drinking coffee in the kitchen. He is wide-awake, and hungrier for company than he knows. He wants to learn what they'll be doing that day. He wants to talk about things, about the day's events and inevitably a longer span of time, the future: "Take each day like your life hangs on it. That's being young, when you can do that, when you're not trapped and have some choice on things." The children are drowsy, but respectful. They go about dressing and taking coffee and doughnuts with him. They are as solicitous as he is. Can they make more coffee? They ask if they can bring him anything—even though they know full well his answer: "No, just yourselves."

Mrs. McCaslin may run the house, but she makes a point of checking every decision with her husband.

He "passes on" even small matters—something connected with one of the children's schoolwork, or a
neighbor's coming visit, or a project for the church.
She is not sly and devious; not clever at appearing
weak but "manipulating" all the while. She genuine-
ly defers to her husband, and his weakness, his illness, his inability to find work—and none of those
new medical, social, or psychological "developments"
have made her see fit to change her ways. Nor is he
inclined to sit back and let the world take *everything*
out of his hands. As a matter of fact, it is interesting
to see how assertive a man and a father he still is,
no matter how awful his fate continues to be. He
is *there,* and always there—in spirit as well as in
body. I have to compare him not only with certain
Negro fathers I know, who hide from welfare
workers and flee their wives and children in fear and
shame and anger, but also with a wide range of
white middle-class fathers who maintain a round-
the-clock absence from home (for business reasons,
for "social" reasons), or else demonstrate a much-
advertised "passivity" while there. Hugh McCaslin,
as poor as one can be in America, not at all well-
educated, jobless, an invalid, and a worried, troubled
man, nevertheless exerts a strong and continuing influence upon everyone in his family. He is, again,
there—not just at home, but very much involved in
almost everything his wife and children do. He
talks a lot. He has strong ideas, and he has a temper.
He takes an interest in all sorts of problems—not
only in those that plague Road's Bend Hollow:

"My daddy was a great talker. He wasn't taken in by

the big people who run this country. He didn't read much, even then when he was young, but he had his beliefs. He said we don't give everyone a break here, and that's against the whole purpose of the country, when it was first settled. You know, there are plenty of people like him. They know how hard it is for a working man to get his share—to get *anything*. Let me tell you, if we had a chance, men like me, we'd vote for a different way of doing things. It just isn't right to use people like they're so much dirt, hire them and fire them and give them no respect and no real security. A few make fortunes and, the rest of us, we're lucky to have our meals from day to day. That's not right; it just isn't.

"I tell my boys not to be fooled. It's tough out there in the world, and it's tough here, too. We've got little here except ourselves. They came in here, the big companies, and bled us dry. They took everything, our coal, our land, our trees, our health. We died like we were in a war, fighting for those companies—and we were lucky to get enough money to bury our kin. They tell me sometimes I'm bitter, my brothers do, but they're just as bitter as I am—they don't talk as much, that's the only difference. Of course it got better here with unions and with some protection the workers got through the government. But you can't protect a man when the company decides to pull out; when it says it's got all it can get, so goodbye folks, and take care of yourselves, because we're moving on to some other place, and we just can't do much more than tell you it was great while it lasted, and you helped us out a lot, yes sir you did."

He does not always talk like that. He can be quiet for long stretches of time, obviously and moodily quiet. His wife finds his silences hard to bear. She doesn't know what they will "lead to." Every day she asks her husband whether there is anything "special" he wants to eat—even though they both

know there isn't much they can afford but the daily
mainstays—bread, coffee, doughnuts, crackers, some
thin stew, potatoes, homemade jam, biscuits. Mrs.
McCaslin defers to her husband, though; one way
is to pay him the courtesy of asking him what he
wants. I have often heard them go back and forth
about food, and as if for all the world they were
far better off, with more choices before them:

"Anything special you want for supper?"

"No. Anything suits me fine. I'm not too hungry."

"Well, if that's it then I'd better make you hungry
with something special."

"What can do that?"

"I thought I'd fry up the potatoes real good tonight and
cut in some onions. It's better than boiling, and I've got
some good pork to throw in. You wait and see."

"I will. It sounds good."

He hurts and she aches for him. His back has its
"bad spells," and she claims her own back can "feel
the pain that goes through his." They don't touch
each other very much in a stranger's presence, or
even, I gather, before their children, but they give
each other long looks of recognition, sympathy, af-
fection, and sometimes anger or worse. They understand each other in that silent, real, lasting way that
defies the gross labels that I and my kind call upon.
It is hard to convey in words—theirs or mine—the
subtle, delicate, largely unspoken, and continual
sense of each other (that is the best that I can do)
that they have. In a gesture, a glance, a frown, a
smile they talk and agree and disagree:

"I can tell what the day will be like for Hugh when he
first gets up. It's all in how he gets out of bed, slow or

with a jump to it. You might say we all have our good days and bad ones, but Hugh has a lot of time to give over to his moods, and around here I guess we're emotional, you might say."

I told her that I thought an outsider like me might not see it that way. She wanted to know what I meant, and I told her: "They call people up in the hollow 'quiet,' and they say they don't show their feelings too much, to each other, let alone in front of someone like me."

"Well, I don't know about that," she answered quickly, a bit piqued. "I don't know what reason they have for that. Maybe they don't have good ears. We don't talk *loud* around here, but we say what's on our mind, straightaway, I believe. I never was one for mincing on words, and I'll tell anyone what's on my mind, be he from around here or way over on the other side of the world. I do believe we're cautious here, and we give a man every break we can, because you don't have it easy around here, no matter who you are; so maybe that's why they think we're not given to getting excited and such. But we do."

I went back to Hugh. Did she think he was more "emotional" than others living nearby?

"Well, I'd say it's hard to say. He has a temper, but I think that goes for all his friends. I think he's about ordinary, only because of his sickness he's likely to feel bad more than some, and it comes out in his moods. You know, when we were married he was the most cheerful man I'd ever met. I mean he smiled all the time, not just because someone said something funny. His daddy told me I was getting the happiest of his kids, and I told him I believed he was right, because I'd already seen it for myself. Today he's his old self sometimes, and I almost don't want to see it, because it makes me think back and remember the good times we had.

"Oh, we have good times now, too; don't mistake me. They just come rare, compared to when times were good. And always it's his pain that hangs over us; we never know when he'll be feeling right, from day to day.

"But when he's got his strength and there's nothing ailing him, he's all set to work, and it gets bad trying to figure what he might do. We talk of moving, but we ask ourselves where we'd go to. We don't want to travel a thousand miles only to be lost in some big city and not have even what we've got. Here there's a neighbor, and our kin, always. We have the house, and we manage to scrape things together, and no one of my kids has ever starved to death. They don't get the food they should, sometimes, but they eat, and they like what I do with food. In fact they complain at church. They say others don't brown the potatoes enough, or the biscuits. And they like a good chocolate cake, and I have that as often as I can.

"When Hugh is low-down he doesn't want to get out of bed, but I make him. He'll sit around and not do much. Every few minutes he'll call my name, but then he won't really have much to say. I have those aspirin, but you can't really afford to use them all the time.

"When he feels good, though, he'll go do chores. He'll make sure we have plenty of water, and he'll cut away some wood and lay it up nearby. He'll walk up the road and see people. He has friends, you know, who aren't sick like him, but it doesn't do them much good around here to be healthy. They can't work any more than Hugh can. It's bad, all the time bad.

"We find our own work, though, and we get paid in the satisfaction you get. We try to keep the house in good shape, and we keep the road clear all year round. That can be a job come winter.

"A lot of the time Hugh says he wished he could read better. He'll get an old magazine—the *Reader's Digest,* or the paper from Charleston—and he'll stay with it for hours. I can see he's having a tough time, but it keeps him busy. He tells the kids to remember his mistakes and not to make them all over again. Then they want to know why he made them. And we're off again. He talks about the coal companies and how they bribed us out of our 'souls,' and how he was a fool, and how it's different now. When they ask what they'll be doing with their reading and writing, it's hard to give them an answer without telling them to move. You don't want to do that, but maybe you do, too. I don't know.

"Hugh fought the television. He said it was no good, and we surely didn't have the money to get one. You can get them real cheap, though, secondhand, and there's a chance to learn how to fix it yourself, because some of the men who come back from the army, they've learned how and they'll teach you and do it for you if you ask them. We had to get one, finally. The kids, they said everyone else didn't have the money, any more than we did, but somehow they got the sets, so why couldn't we? That started something, all right. Hugh wanted to know if they thought we could manufacture money. So they wanted to know how the others got their sets. And Hugh said he didn't know, but if they would go find out, and come tell him, why then he'd show them that each family is different, and you can't compare people like that. Well, then they mentioned it to their uncle—he works down there in the school, keeping it in order, and he's on a regular salary, you know, and lives as good as anyone around here, all things told, I'd say. So he came and told us he'd do it, get a set for us, because the kids really need them. They feel left out without TV.

"That got Hugh going real bad. He didn't see why the radio wasn't enough, and he wasn't going to take and take and take. He wanted help, but not for a TV set. And then he'd get going on the coal companies, and how we got that radio for cash, and it was brand-new and expensive, but he was making plenty of money then. And he didn't want to go begging, even from kin. And we could just do without, so long as we eat and have a place to sleep and no one's at our door trying to drive us away or take us to jail.

"Finally I had to say something. I had to. It was one of the hardest things I've ever had to do. He was getting worse and worse, and the kids they began to think he was wrong in the head over a thing like TV, and they didn't know why; they couldn't figure it out. He said they wouldn't see anything but a lot of trash, and why should we let it all come in here like that? And he said they'd lose interest in school, and become hypnotized or something, and he'd read someplace it happens. And he said gadgets and machines, they came cheap, but you end up losing a lot more than you get, and that was what's happening in America today.

"Now, the kids could listen for so long, and they're respectful to him, to both of us, I think you'll agree. They'd try to answer him, real quiet, and say it wasn't so important, TV wasn't, it was just there to look at, and we would all do it and have a good time. And everyone was having it, but that didn't mean that the world was changing, or that you'd lose anything just because you looked at a picture every once in a while.

"And finally, as I say, I joined in. I had to—and I sided with them. I said they weren't going to spend their lives looking at TV, no sir, but it would be O.K. with me if we had it in the house, that I could live with it, and I think we could all live with it. And Hugh, he just looked at me and didn't say another word, not that day or any other afterwards until much later on, when we had the set already, and he would look at the news and listen real careful to what they tell you might be happening. He told me one day, it was a foolish fight we all had, and television wasn't any better or worse than a lot of other things. But he wished the country would make more than cheap TVs. 'We could all live without TV if we had something more to look forward to,' he said. I couldn't say anything back. He just wasn't feeling good that day, and to tell the truth TV is good for him when he's like that, regardless of what he says. He watches it like he used to listen to his radio, and he likes it better than he'd ever admit to himself, I'm sure."

On Sundays they go to church. Hugh says he doesn't much believe in "anything," but he goes; he stays home only when he doesn't feel good, not out of any objection to prayer. They all have their Sunday clothes, and they all enjoy getting into them. They become new and different people. They walk together down the hollow and along the road that takes them to a Baptist church. They worship vigorously and sincerely, and with a mixture of awe, bravado, passion, and restraint that leaves an outside observer feeling, well—skeptical, envious, surprised, mystified, admiring, and vaguely nostalgic. I think they emerge much stronger and more united for the experience, and with as much "perspective," I suppose, as others get from different forms of contemplation, submission, and joint participation. Hugh can be as stoical as anyone else, and in church his stoicism can simply pour out. The world *is* confusing, you see. People have *always* suffered, good people. Somewhere, somehow, it is not all for naught—but that doesn't mean one should raise one's hopes too high, not on this earth. After church there is "socializing," and its importance need not be stressed in our self-conscious age of "groups" that solve "problems" or merely facilitate "interaction." When I have asked myself what "goes on" in those "coffee periods," I remind myself that I heard a lot of people laughing, exchanging news, offering greetings, expressing wishes, fears, congratulations and condolences. I think there is a particular warmth and intensity to some of the meetings because, after all, people do not see much of one another during the week. Yet how many residents of our cities or our suburbs see one another as regularly as these "isolated" people do? Hugh McCaslin put it quite forcefully: "We may not see much of anyone for a few days, but Sunday will come and we see everyone we want to see, and by the time we go home we know everything there is to know." As some of us say, they "communicate efficiently."

There is, I think, a certain hunger for companionship that builds up even among people who do not feel as "solitary" as some of their observers have considered them. Particularly at night one feels the woods and the hills close in on "the world." The McCaslins live high up in a hollow, but they don't have a "view." Trees tower over their cabin, and the smoke rising from their chimney has no space at all to dominate. When dusk comes there are no lights to be seen, only their lights to turn on. In winter they eat at about 5 and they are in bed about 7:30 or 8. The last hour before bed is an almost formal time. Every evening Mr. McCaslin smokes his pipe and either reads or carves wood. Mrs. McCaslin has finished putting things away after supper and sits sewing—"mending things and fixing things;

there isn't a day goes by that something doesn't tear." The children watch television. They have done what homework they have (or are willing to do) before supper. I have never heard them reprimanded for failing to study. Their parents tell them to go to school; to stay in school; to do well in school—but they aren't exactly sure it makes much difference. They ask the young to study, but I believe it is against their "beliefs" to say one thing and mean another, to children or anyone else.

In a sense, then, they are blunt and truthful with each other. They say what they think, but worry about how to say what they think so that the listener remains a friend or—rather often—a friendly relative. Before going to bed they say good-night, and one can almost feel the reassurance that goes with the greeting. It is very silent "out there" or "outside."

"Yes, I think we have good manners," Hugh McCaslin once told me. "It's a tradition, I guess, and goes back to Scotland, or so my daddy told me. I tell the kids that they'll know a lot more than I do when they grow up, or I hope they will; but I don't believe they'll have more consideration for people—no sir. We teach them to say hello in the morning, to say good morning, like you said. I know it may not be necessary, but it's good for people living real close to be respectful of one another. And the same goes for the evening.

"Now, there'll be fights. You've seen us take after one another. That's O.K. But we settle things on the same day, and we try not to carry grudges. How can you carry a grudge when you're just this one family here, and miles away from the next one? Oh, I know it's natural to be spiteful and carry a grudge. But you can only carry it so far, that's what I say. Carry it until the sun goes down, then wipe the slate clean and get ready for another day. I say that a lot to the kids."

Once I went with the McCaslins to a funeral. A great-uncle of Mrs. McCaslin's had died at 72. He happened to be a favorite of hers and of her mother. They lived much nearer to a town than the McCaslins do, and were rather well-to-do. He had worked for the county government all his life—in the Appalachian region, no small position. The body lay at rest in a small church, with hand-picked flowers in bunches around it. A real clan had gathered from all over, as well as friends. Of course it was a sad occasion, despite the man's advanced age; yet even so I was struck by the restraint of the people, their politeness to one another, no matter how close or "near kin" they were. For a moment I watched them move about and tried to block off their subdued talk from my brain. It occurred to me that, were they dressed differently and in a large manor home, they might very much resemble English gentry at a reception. They were courtly people; they looked it and acted it. Many were tall, thin, and close-mouthed. A few were potbellied, as indeed befits a good lusty duke or duchess. They could smile and even break out into a laugh, but it was always noticeable when it happened. In general they were not exactly demonstrative or talkative, yet they were clearly interested in one another and had very definite and strong sentiments, feelings, emotions, whatever. In other words, as befits the gentry, they had feelings but had them under "appropriate" control.

They also seemed suitably resigned, or philosophical
—as the circumstances warranted. What crying there
was, had already been done. There were no out-
bursts of any kind, and no joviality either. It was
not a wake.

A few days later Hugh McCaslin of Road's Bend
Hollow talked about the funeral and life and death:

"He probably went too early, from what I hear. He was
in good health, and around here you either die very young
—for lack of a doctor—or you really last long. That's the
rule, though I admit we have people live to all ages, like
being sick as I am. It happens to you, and you know it,
but that's O.K. When I was a boy I recall my people bury-
ing their old people, right near where we lived. We had a
little graveyard, and we used to know all our dead people
pretty well. You know, we'd play near their graves, and go
ask our mother or daddy about who this one was and what
he did, and like that. The other way was through the Bible:
Everything was written down on pieces of paper inside the
family Bible. There'd be births and marriages and deaths,
going way back, I guess as far back as the beginning of the
country. I'm not sure of the exact time, but a couple of
hundred years, easy.

"We don't do that now—it's probably one of the biggest
changes, maybe. I mean apart from television and things
like that. We're still religious, but we don't keep the
records, and we don't bury our dead nearby. It's just not
that much of a *home* here, a place that you have and your
kin always had and your children and theirs will have, until
the end of time, when God calls us all to account. This here
place—it's a good house, mind you—but it's just a place I
got. A neighbor of my daddy's had it, and he left it, and my
daddy heard and I came and fixed it up and we have it
for nothing. We worked hard and put a lot into it, and
we treasure it, but it never was a *home*, not the kind I

knew, and my wife did. We came back to the hollow, but it wasn't like it used to be when we were kids and you felt you were living in the same place all your ancestors did. We're *part* of this land, we were here to start and we'll probably see it die, me or my kids will, the way things are going. There will be no one left here and the stripminers will kill every good acre we have. I thought of that at the funeral. I thought maybe it's just as well to die now, if everything's headed in that direction. I guess that's what happens at a funeral. You get to thinking."

June 1968

FURTHER READING SUGGESTED BY THE AUTHOR:

Night Comes to the Cumberland by Harry M. Caudill (Boston: Little, Brown & Co., 1963). A first-rate general historical account of the problems that plague Appalachia; probably the best known contemporary work.

Stinking Creek by John Fetterman (New York: E. P. Dutton & Co., 1967). A careful description of one hollow, sensitively done with great candor and honesty.

Yesterday's People by Jack A. Weller (Lexington, Ky.: University of Kentucky Press, 1965). A minister's social and cultural observations, along with some accurate, thoughtful, and properly ambiguous conclusions.

On the Case
in Resurrection City

CHARLAYNE HUNTER

Resurrection City—where the poor had hoped to become visible and effective—is dead. And despite the contention of many people, both black and white, that it should never have been born, R.C. was, as its City Fathers had been quick to point out, a moment in history that may yet have a telling effect on the future of this country. For although Resurrection City was never really a city, per se, it functioned as a city, with all the elements of conflict that arise when public issues and private troubles come together.

The public issues were clear and could be articulated—at least in a general way—by most of the people who lived there. Handbills had helped residents formulate their statement of purpose. "What will the Poor People's Campaign do in Washington?" read one handbill. "We will build powerful nonviolent demonstrations on the issues of jobs, income, welfare, health, housing, human rights. These massive demonstrations will be aimed at government centers of power and they will be expanded if necessary. We must

61

make the government face up to poverty and racism." If such a statement was not specific enough, residents—who in all probability found it difficult to always know just what the leaders had in mind (as did the leaders themselves)— would simply fend off the question with a statement like, "*We* know what the demands are." If pressed further, they would glare accusingly at the questioner, as if to further confirm his ignorance. (This technique of bluffing one's way into the offensive was initiated by the leader of the Poor People's Campaign, the Rev. Ralph Abernathy. The press was relentless in its efforts to get Mr. Abernathy to give out more specifics about his demands, but this was impossible for a long while simply because none had been formulated.)

The private troubles of those who came to live in R.C. were less clear, at least in the beginning. And as these troubles emerged—sometimes in the form of fights, rapes, thefts, and harassment—they became far more prominent than the cause or the individuals who came to fight for it. The outside world concerned itself with the disorganization and lack of leadership in the camp. And while this was certainly a valid concern, critics seemed to be missing one essential point—that the life styles of the poor vary, from individual to individual and from region to region. Long before coming to Resurrection City, leaders and followers had been conditioned by their backgrounds and the life styles they had established. That is why, for example, the first City Manager of R.C., Jesse Jackson—a 26-year-old Chicagoan and an official of the Southern Christian Leadership Conference (S.C.L.C.)—had more success with the Northern urban hustler than did Hosea Williams, the second City Manager, who came out of the South and had much more success with diffident rural blacks.

Most of the conflicts at the camp were caused by the ghetto youths whose lives in the asphalt jungles of the North led them to view Resurrection City as a camp-outing and an alfresco frolic. Surrounded by trees, grass, and open air, the Northern youths were among alien things, which (before the rain and mud) were hostile to them. The innocence of their Southern counterparts—for whom the trees, grass, open air, and mud are a way of life—was a challenge to the Northerners. With such easy, church-oriented prey, the hip cat from the North immediately went into his thing—taking advantage of the uninitiated. Southerners had the history of the movement behind them. They had produced the sit-ins, the Freedom Rides, the Bus Boycotts—the 1960's Direct Action Task Force. And yet much of the Southern mystique got beaten by the hard, hostile life style of the urban ghetto-dweller.

No one is quite sure how many people moved into Resurrection City, although there was an attempt to register people as they came in. The registration count was 6312, but the community was nothing if not mobile and there was no way to count the outflow.

The people came to the District from all sections of the country. They came in bus caravans and on trains. Some came from the South in the Mule Train (which was put into a regular train in Atlanta because the horses were giving out), some came from the nearby North in cars or on foot. They came representing the church. They came representing the community. They came representing street gangs—those that would fight and those that wouldn't. And many came representing themselves. Most came as followers. But, of necessity, a few emerged as leaders. Many came to participate in the campaign for as long as S.C.L.C. wanted them there, and then they planned to go home. Others came thinking of the North as a land of opportunity. And *they* came to stay forever.

Today, the site where Resurrection City stood is cleared. After the sun baked the mud dry, patches of growing grass were placed there, and although the land is not quite so green as it was before, it is just as it was when the architects began designing Resurrection City on paper back in April. Perhaps if they had it to do over, they

would change a few things, because, by now, they would
have learned about the differences in poverty—that poor
people do not automatically respond positively to one another.

The design, on paper, had been impressive. Three architects (none of them Negroes), with the help of students of the Howard University School of Architecture
(all of them Negroes), produced plans that called for
modest A-frame structures, which could be built small
enough for two and large enough for six or eight and
which would house 3000 people for two to four months.
The prefabricated units—25 percent of them A-frames
and 75 percent of them dormitories—were to be assembled
in Virginia by local white volunteers, then brought to
Washington in trucks that would be unloaded next to
the building sites, starting west and building eastward.

By the time the first stake for an A-frame was driven
in by Mr. Abernathy, around a thousand people had already come into Washington and had been housed in
coliseums and churches.

During the first week, morale and energy and activity
levels were high. But one of the first indications that the
paper plans might not succeed came when the New York
delegation insisted upon setting up shop in the most
easternward section of the site. New Yorkers, independent, fast-paced, and accustomed to protests (like rent
strikes) that require organization, were going to do things
their own way. Though this meant that they had to carry
their own wood all the way from the front of the site to
the back, they set up their structures with record-breaking
speed. Where it sometimes took three men working together an hour to put up an A-frame, in the New York
contingent three men produced an A-frame in 15 minutes.
There was, among *everyone,* a feeling of distrust for larger
communities: Provincialism had reared its head.

After a week and a half of more or less organized en-
deavor, there followed a long stretch of bad weather. It

rained every day, and rivers of thick, brown mud stood in doorways and flowed along the walkways from one end of the camp to the other. But although the mud and rain sapped some of the energy of some of the assemblers, it seemed to inspire creativity in others—the majority, in fact, since they were eager to get their houses built so that they could move in. More people came to R.C. than left. And although many had been evacuated to churches and schools—often long distances away—the Mexican-Americans and the Indians were the only contingents that chose to stay on high ground.

When the rains did not let up, the last vestiges of formal organization at R.C. slid unceremoniously into the mud. But those who had left returned, and others joined them, and all waded through. Wood that had been lost turned up as porches for the A-frame houses—luxuries not called for in the paper plans. "It was interesting to see this mass-produced, prefab stuff developing into color and rambunctiousness," one of the planners said.

By the time most of the A-frames had been filled, what existed on the site of the planned city was a camp rather than a community, with some areas so compounded with picket fences or solid fences that no outsider could get in. Walking or wading through the camp, one saw not only simple, unadorned A-frames, but split-levels and duplexes. Some were unpainted; others were painted simply (usually with yellows and burgundy); and still others were both mildly and wildly, reverently and irreverently, decorated with slogans. One house bore on its side a verse from the Bible: "And they said one to another, behold, this dreamer cometh. Come now therefore, and let us slay him, and cast him into some pit, and we will say, some evil beast hath devoured him: and we shall see what will become of his dreams. Genesis 37. Martin Luther King, Jr., 1929-1968." Others had such slogans as "Black Power on Time," "Soul Power," "United People Power, Toledo, Ohio," "Soul City, U.S.A.," and "The Dirty Dozen," on a building I figured was a dormitory. And, of course, the inevitable "Flower Power." "I Have a Dream" stickers appeared in most places, as well as pictures of Martin Luther King—usually enshrined beside the. canvas-and-wood cots inside the houses.

Just as the slogans varied widely, so did the inside appearance of the houses. While many looked like the wreck of the Hesperus, in others, by 9 A.M. when the camp was opened to visitors, beds were made, clothes were hung, floors were swept, and—in several houses—plank coffee-tables were adorned with greenery in tin-can vases.

The Coretta King Day Care Center was perhaps the most successful unit in the camp. A local church group contributed most of the materials, including books like *Alice in Wonderland, What Are You Looking At?, The Enormous Egg.* and Bennett Cerf's *Pop-Up Lyrics.* There were even toy cars and trucks, water colors, and jigsaw puzzles. And a hundred pairs of muddy boots. The children played games and sang songs such as "If You're Happy and You Know It, Clap Your Hands" and, of course, "We Shall Overcome." And they went on field trips—to the Smithsonian, the National Historical Wax Museum, and Georgetown University. Enrollment was about 75.

Altogether, Resurrection City never contained more than the average American city—the bare-bone necessities. Still, many people received more medical attention than ever before in their lives. A young mother left Marks, Miss., with a baby whose chances of survival, she had been told, were very slim. He was dying of malnutrition. After three weeks of medical care—vitamins, milk, food—he began gaining weight and life. For others, teeth were saved. Upper-respiratory infections—at one point a source of alarm to those outside the camp—were treated and curbed. And when one of the residents died while on a demonstration in the food line at the Agriculture Department, there was little doubt that it was not Resurrection City that killed him, but the lack of adequate medical attention back home. Most of the residents were also eating better. The menus were often a hodge-podge affair—sometimes consisting of beef stew, turnip greens, apple sauce, and an orange—but the food was nutritious. And you did not need food stamps to get it.

Residents of Resurrection City found it difficult to understand the outside world's reaction via the press to conditions within the camp. The stink from the toilets that filled one's nostrils whenever a breeze stirred was, as one observer put it, "the smell of poverty." Residents put it another way. "I appreciate the mud," a woman from Detroit said. "It might help get some of this disease out."

The mud of Resurrection City was seen by many as unifying, if not cleansing. Andy Young, an S.C.L.C. executive, trying to dispel rumors of disorganization in the camp, said one day: "We are a movement, not an organization. And we move when the spirit says move. Anything outside is God's business. We are incorporated by the Lord and baptized by all this rain."

While the camp was virtually leaderless from a formal, organizational standpoint (Mr. Abernathy was always off traveling with a large entourage of S.C.L.C. officials), it did not lack individual movers and doers. One day, a discussion of the mud revealed such a person. Standing attentively at a press conference on a sunny day, with an umbrella over her head, Mrs. Lila Mae Brooks of Sunflower County, Miss., said, to no one in particular, "We used to mud and us who have commodes are used to no sewers." A tall, thin, spirited woman, Mrs. Brooks talks with little or no prompting. Observing that I was interested, she went on: "We used to being sick, too. And we used to death. All my children [she has eight] born sickly. But in Sunflower County, sick folks sent from the hospital and told to come back in two months. They set up 27 rent houses—rent for $25—and they put you out when you don't pay. People got the health department over 'bout the sewers, but Mayor said they couldn't put in sewers until 1972." She is 47, and for years has worked in private homes, cotton fields, and churches. In 1964 she was fired from a job for helping Negroes register to vote. For a while, she was on the S.C.L.C. staff, teaching citizenship. When she had a sunstroke, and later a heart attack, she had to go on welfare. (She is also divorced.) For three years, she got $40-a-month child support, and finally $73. She left her children with her mother, who is 80, and sister to come to the campaign.

"People in Sunflower asked my friends was I sick 'cause they hadn't seen me. Then they saw me on TV in Washington and said I'd better head back before the first or they'd cut off my welfare check. You go out the state overnight and they cut off your welfare check. But that's OK. I had to come. When S.C.L.C. chose me from Eastland's County, he met his match. I've seen so much. I've seen 'em selling food stamps and they tell you if you don't buy, they cut off your welfare check. And that stuff they sell there don't count—milk, tobacco, and washing powder. Well, how you gonna keep clean? All the welfare people know is what *they* need. I ain't raising no more white babies for them. Ain't goin' that road no more. I drug my own children through the cotton fields, now they talkin' 'bout not lettin' us go to Congress. Well, I'll stand on Eastland's toes. People from 12 months to 12 months without work. People with no money. Where the hell the money at? I say to myself, I'll go to Washington and find out. Talking about using it to build clinics. Then they make people pay so much at the clinics they get turned away. What the people gettin' ain't enough to say grace over. I done wrote to Washington so much they don't have to ask my name."

I asked Mrs. Brooks how long she planned to say here. "I don't know, honey," she said as she put her sunglasses on. "They just might have to 'posit my body in Washington."

There were other women organizing welfare groups and working in the lunch halls, and still others, like Miss Muriel Johnson, a social worker on loan to S.C.L.C. from other organizations. This was her first movement and she was in charge of holding "sensitivity" sessions. When I asked her what a sensitivity session was, she said, "Well, you just can't take a bunch of people out and march them down Independence Avenue. All they know is that they're hungry and want something done about it. We got 150 to 200 people out a day into nonviolent demonstrations. We got to teach them to protect themselves and prepare for whatever. We have to explain situations to people. And we have to talk with them, not down to them. If they get something out of this training, they'll go home and do something."

Joining Mrs. Brooks and Miss Johnson were many other young men and women, among them college students who, like the students of the old movement (the early 1960s), believed that it was better for black boys and girls to give themselves immediately and fully to a worthwhile cause than to finish college. Many of them wore their hair natural and some wore buttons that said, "Doing it black." Young men like Leon and J.T., both S.C.L.C. organizers in the South, held no place in the movement hierarchy, but were, as the residents were fond of saying of anybody plugged in to what was going on, "on the case."

Leon and J.T. led demonstrations and boosted morale by taking part in the day-to-day problems and activities of Resurrection City. The difference between them and many of the other S.C.L.C. officials was that when R.C. residents were tired and smelly from marching eight miles to a demonstration and back, so were Leon and J.T. When residents went to bed wearing all their clothes and wrapped in blankets saturated with dampness, so did Leon and J.T. And if Leon and J.T. could still sing freedom songs the next day, then so could they. There were not, however, enough Leons and J.T.s. Many weeks had been spent building the Abernathy compound—a large frame structure surrounded by A-frames for his aides. But despite a ceremonial gesture of walking in with a suitcase and announcing that he was moving in, Mr. Abernathy never lived in R.C. Nor did his lieutenants.

One of the most effective communicators around Resurrection City was a man of a different breed from that of Leon or J.T.: Lance Watson, better (and perhaps solely) known as Sweet Willie Wine. Sweet Willie, 29, is the leader of the Memphis Invaders, the group accused of starting the riots in Memphis after the assassination of Martin Luther King. (Sweet Willie denies this.) He spent most of his time walking around the camp, wrapped in a colorful serapi, combing his heavy Afro. He condemns the Vietnam war as immoral, and of his own time in the army paratroops says, "In service I took the great white father's word. I thought it was all right to be half a man. Now it is time to question. We are questioning everything now."

When the campaign was over, most of the Invaders went home. Sweet Willie, however, is still walking the streets of Washington, occasionally plugging in to local militants, but more often holding down some corner in the black ghetto.

The Invaders bridged the gap between the diffident Southern blacks and the hustling ghetto youth from the North. Memphis, after all, is a kind of half-way place, with elements both of the Southern rural and the urban ghetto scenes. And it is perhaps because of this that they made it through to the end. The Blackstone Rangers, from Chicago, did not. Early on, they were sent home for causing trouble. Acting on the theory that if the tough guys were used as peace officers, they would be too busy keeping others out of trouble to get in trouble themselves, S.C.L.C. officials began using the Blackstone Rangers as marshals. It didn't work.

Yet most of the gangs there saw themselves more as protectors of the other black people in the camp than as participants in the campaign. The leader of St. Louis's Zulu 1200's, Clarence Guthrie, said that the Zulus did not pretend to be nonviolent, but "since this campaign concerns a lot of brothers and sisters who are working their thing, we'll use our resources to protect them."

With so many disparate elements in the camp, it only took a slight incident to cause a large group to assemble, with a great deal of fight potential. Most of the Southerners had come with an S.C.L.C. orientation, and as a result they were still singing "We Shall Overcome," including the verse "Black and white together." But few people from above the Mason-Dixon line were singing "We Shall Overcome," let alone "Black and white together." They usually ignored the whites inside the camp, who for the most part were either kids who would do all the dirty work or hippies off somewhere by themselves with their flowers. Still, any altercation outside the camp usually involved some white person. Such was the case when a fight broke out just outside the grounds. Police— mostly whites—appeared in large numbers. The Tent City Rangers, a group of older men formed as security officers, broke up the fight, but some of the boys whose adrenaline had risen headed for a white man wearing bermuda shorts and taking pictures. With dispatch, they relieved him of his camera and disappeared. The man wanted his camera back, he said, because it was expensive. But he added, "I think I understand. I come down here in my bermuda shorts taking pictures. And I guess I understand how this would make them angry."

Laurice Barksdale, a 24-year-old veteran from Atlanta, was angry, too. But he vented his frustrations in another way. From early in the morning to late in the afternoon, the sweet smell of baking bread joined the other scents in the air. In a small A-frame decorated with the motto "Unhung-up Bread," Barksdale spent every day baking bread for residents and visitors as well. The supplies had come from a white New Yorker who travels from community to community teaching people how to make bread. At R.C. he discovered Barksdale, who had learned to cook in his high school home-economics class, and set him up in business. After four years in the Marines, Barksdale had come home to Atlanta and had not been able to find a job. His mother, who worked for S.C.L.C., suggested that he go along on the Poor People's Campaign to see if he could help out. Barksdale says he's not really interested in making money. "I got a cause," he says. "And a lot of brothers and sisters around me."

The one S.C.L.C. higher-up always on the case was Hosea Williams, who early in the campaign became the City Manager. One of Hosea's major assets was the gift of rap.

One Sunday morning he was stopped by three well-dressed white men, one of whom said he was running for Congress from Florida and had come to R.C. because he felt he and his people ought to know about it. Soon after the conversation began, the man asked Hosea about his background, and if he was a Communist. Hosea was not offended by the question, but moved into it slowly. He denied being a Communist.

"What is Resurrection City all about?" Hosea asked rhetorically. "This is what you have to know. We are asking for jobs. Not welfare. Check the cat on the welfare rolls and you'll find his mother and daddy were on welfare.

"What we've got to have is a redefinition of work. As Lillian Smith indicated in her book, I think *Killers of the Dream,* what we have is a conflicting ideology in our value system. The reason I loved Dr. King was that he made $600,000 in one year and died a pauper. We have got to let scientists go to work and create jobs. I know it can be done. I was working as a research chemist for 14 years trying to rid this country of insects. I was born in Attapulgus, Ga. My father was a field hand and my mother worked in the white folks' house. I raised myself while she raised the white folks' children. And we got to get some help for the old. And we got to do something about this educational system. That's what produced the hippies. White colleges. I got more respect for the hippies than I have for the hypocrites.

"R.C. is just a place we have to sleep and get some food to fight a war—a nonviolent war. We are here for an economic bill of rights. Congress's job is to solve the problems. We are political analysts and psychiatrists and Congress is the patient."

On that Sunday morning there was a sense of movement and activity throughout the camp. This was true on any given day. Near the entrance to the camp, young boys played checkers and whist, and some were getting haircuts. Over the P.A. system in City Hall, someone was calling for attention. "Will Cornbread please report to City Hall immediately? Attention. Will Cornbread please report to City Hall immediately?" Like Leon and J.T. most people didn't know any other name for Cornbread but Cornbread. But Cornbread was a household word because he was on the case.

Also on that morning, a tall, thin, white man looking like the church pictures of Jesus took up a position behind a table near the checkers game and began making predictions—that there would be a big snow in August; that there would be a Republican President in 1972; that people of America would one day eat one another.

"Are you open to question?" someone called out. He did not respond.

The thin man continued, saying that he had prophesied the burning in Washington. He was interrupted again, by another voice from what had become a building crowd. "Tell me what the number gon' be so I can be a rich man tomorrow." An elderly Negro man with a pair of crutches next to his chair called out, to no one in particular, "Hey, where are my cigars?"

I asked the crippled man where he came from. Coy, Ala. How long had he been at R.C.? "Since they drove the first nail," he answered. "What have you been doing?" "Well, I can't do much. I've got arthritis. I usually get up about 4 A.M. and just sit here. But I tried to organize a men's Bible class like at my church back home. Not too much success, though. I had a lovely time yesterday. Seven of us went out to a church and we had services. Then we had a wonderful dinner there—fried chicken, candied potatoes, and wrinkle steaks. You know what those are, don't you?" He smiled. "If I can hop a ride, I want to go back."

Sitting behind him were two young men. One was saying, "I got to fly home to court tomorrow. Charge of marihuana. Ain't had none." The young man was from New York. It was not the kind of thing one was likely to hear from his Southern counterpart. Narcotics is the traditional way out for many of the frustrated young in the asphalt jungles of the North. Somehow, this syndrome never hit the South. A young Southern black, eager to escape the lot of his father, has one way out—the army. And many of them, once they enlist, choose to stay.

Soon another announcement came over the P.A. system asking all residents who planned to take part in the day's demonstrations to report to the front gate.

On Sundays, Resurrection City—with all its diversity— was opened up to even more diversity. Sunday was tourist day and visitors began arriving sometime after breakfast. One particular Sunday, as the residents drifted out of the front gate to a demonstration, among the tourists coming in were many well-dressed Negroes from the District on their way home from church or elsewhere (as remote as they seemed to be from things, it didn't seem likely that they would have dressed up to come to R.C.). Some whites came, too. Mainly the tourists drove by in cars, slowing down long enough to snap a picture and continue on. To the Negro visitors (who almost never wore boots to protect their shoes from the mud), most residents (who did wear boots and slept in them at night to keep warm) were cordial, sometimes condescending (something of a unique turnabout in the scheme of things)—"Yes, *do* come in and have a look around. We're right proud of what we have here." Later, at a Lou Rawls concert, which was inadvertently set up before the demonstration, but which Hosea decided to let go on, Hosea addressed the crowd and concluded with a few well-chosen words for the Negro tourists: "The police want to use those billy clubs. But they ain't gonna bother you today. Today is Uncle Tom Day, and they don't whip up on Uncle Tom heads."

Demonstrations were the one constant in R.C. Each demonstration I attended was different from another, not so much because the body of demonstrators changed as because of their usual tendency to "do what the spirit say do."

Although R.C. residents had been there before—to present demands for changes in the welfare system—my first demonstration was at the Department of Health, Education, and Welfare. The 200 demonstrators marched into the auditorium of the building and sent word that they wanted to see "Brother Cohen"—Wilbur J. Cohen, Secretary of Health, Education, and Welfare. An otherwise impressive delegation—including Assistant Secretary Ralph K. Huitt and Harold Howe II of H.E.W.'s Office of Education—was sent in, but was given short shrift. Led by Hosea, the demonstrators began to chant "We want Cohen," and Hosea turned from the second-string officials and told the crowd: "You might as well get comfortable," and before he had finished a young boy in gray trousers and a green shirt had taken off his tennis shoes, rolled up his soiled brown jacket into a headrest, and stretched out on the floor. As he closed his eyes, the crowd, led by Hosea, began singing "Woke Up This Morning With My Mind Set on Freedom." In between songs the crowd would chant "We want Cohen." An elderly lady from New Orleans, who after the march obviously had little strength left to stand and yell and chant, simply shook her head in time with whatever she happened to be hearing at the moment.

The more pressure the officials put upon Hosea to relent, the stronger the support from the crowd. Given the demonstrators' vote of confidence, he began to rap. "I never lived in a democracy until I moved to Resurrection City. But it looks like the stuff is all right."

"Sock soul, brother!" the people yelled.

"Out here," he continued, "they got the gray matter to discover a cure for cancer, but can't."

"Sock soul, brother!"

Then, to the tune of the song "Ain't Gonna Let Nobody Turn Me 'Round," Hosea led the group in singing, "Ain't Gonna Let the Lack of Health Facilities Turn Me 'Round." And at the end of the song—something like three hours after the demonstrators had demanded to see Cohen—the word spread through the auditorium: "Cohen's on the case."

Demonstrators who had spread throughout the building buttonholing anybody and everybody who looked important, demanding that they "go downstairs and get Cohen," filed back into the auditorium. And as Cohen appeared, an exultant cheer rose from the demonstrators—not for Cohen but for the point that they had won.

Before Cohen spoke, Huitt came to the microphone. He looked relieved. "I'd just like to say, before introducing the Secretary, that I haven't heard preaching and singing like that since I was a boy. Maybe that's what wrong with me." The crowd liked that and showed it. "Get on the case, brother," someone called. And as clenched black fists went into the air—a gesture that had come to stand for "Silence!" and succeeded in getting it—Cohen spoke:

"Welcome to your auditorium," he said, managing a smile. He proceeded to outline his response to the demonstrators' demands, which included changing the state-by-state system of welfare to a federally controlled one. When he had finished, he introduced a very polished, gray-haired, white matron sitting next to him as "our director of civil rights." A voice of a Negro woman in rags called out to her: "Get to work, baby."

The second demonstration I attended was at the Justice Department. Earlier in the day, as rumors grew of dissension between the Mexican-Americans and the blacks, Reiss Tiejerina, the leader of the Mexican-Americans, and Rodolfo ("Corky") Gonzales, his fiery lieutenant, appeared for a press conference to be held jointly with Hosea and the Indian leader, Hank Adams. Accompanying Tiejerina and Gonzales was a small contingent of Mexican-Americans with unmuddied feet (during the entire campaign, their group remained in the Hawthorne School, where there was not only hot food but hot showers as well), and a few Indians. Tiejerina had one major concern: regaining the land in New Mexico that, he claims, was illegally taken away from his people some 300 years ago in the Treaty of Guadalupe Hidalgo.

As the press conference broke up and the demonstrators made ready for the march, the Mexican-Americans boarded buses to take them to the Justice Department, while the preparations of the blacks consisted of a black demonstrator's shouting: "Get your feet in the street. We're marching today."

The Justice Department demonstration was officially under the direction of Corky Gonzales. His demands were that the Attorney General speak with 100 of the demonstrators, with all ethnic groups represented equally—which turned out to be 25 Mexican-Americans, 15 Indians, 20 poor whites, and 40 blacks. The Attorney General agreed to speak with only 20 of the demonstrators, and this proved totally unacceptable to Gonzales. (Tiejerina was not there at the time.)

For several days, talk of getting arrested in some demonstration had become intense. Somehow, as the hours wore on during the Justice Department demonstration, it was decided that this might be the place. The question seemed to be, was it the time and was the cause broad enough?

There were some demonstrators who came prepared for any eventuality, regardless of the cause. As long as the order came from S.C.L.C. Ben Ownes, 52, widely known as Sunshine, was prepared. The crowd blocking the entrance to the Justice Department (a federal offense in itself), though led by Gonzales, was singing the S.C.L.C. songs: To the tune of "No More Weepin', No More Mourning," they sang, "No More Broken Treaties. . . ." Sunshine talked about his involvement in the movement.

"In Birmingham, in 1963, friends from my church were picketing. I went down. I didn't tote no signs, but my boss still told me when I got back to work not to tote. Then next time I went and toted. The third time I toted, I didn't have a job. But I'd heap more rather work for Dr. King for $25 a week than for $125. My house has been threatened. My mother has been threatened. But I registered a lot of people in Selma, Green County, Sumter County, and many others. Sometime I be sick, but I can't go home. I've gone too far now to turn 'round. I've been so close to so many things. Jimmy Lee Jackson got killed. James Reed got beat to death. Mrs. Liuzzo killed. September 15, 1963, six people were killed—two boys and four girls. If I die for *something* I don't mind. I've been in jail 17 or 18 times. But we really got to work in this town."

The police, however, did not seem to be in an arresting mood. They just stood in the street behind the demonstrators, more or less impassive. Suddenly Hosea took the bullhorn.

"Look at those cops!" he shouted.

The crowd turned. The cops shifted uneasily. "You see what they've done," he continued, his voice rising. The crowd looked. "They don't have on their badges, so that when they take you to jail and do whatever they're gon' do to you, you won't be able to identify them." The crowd was now facing the policemen and could see that not one of them was wearing a badge. Hosea started to rap about police brutality and the sickness of America. "Just look at that!" he cried, pointing an accusing finger. And no one had to be told, this time, what they were looking for. All could see that the shiny badges had been put back in their places—on the chests of the entire cadre of policemen standing behind them. But Hosea was now into his thing. "But look," he said, again pointing. "Just to show you how sick this country is—the sickness of America and racism—*look*." The crowd was baffled. What was he talking about now? Hosea, virtually overcome with rage, now shouted, "You see how sick this country is? Otherwise how come all the white cops are lined up on one side and all the black cops lined up further down the street? Just look at it!" The division in the line was distinct. Immediately behind the demonstrators was a line of white policemen. To the extreme left of the demonstrators a solid line of black faces in uniform. Hosea rapped a good long while.

As the evening wore on, and the Attorney General did not show up and the demonstrators did not get arrested, there seemed to be some indecision among the demonstration's leaders. Hosea, at times, seemed at a loss. Corky had tired of leading the group in songs, and the demonstrators had never quite caught all the words. Corky and Hosea huddled often, only to return and lead more singing. Father James Groppi of Milwaukee showed up, received wide applause, made an impassioned speech, and joined in the singing. At one point, Hosea broke off to consult with his lawyer, and Tiejerina showed up. "What's going on?" he asked innocently. Hosea explained that the Attorney General had refused to see 100, but would see 20. "That's fine. O.K., isn't it? We send the 20?"

Hosea looked confused. "Corky is holding out for 100." "I will talk to Corky," Tiejerina said, and good-naturedly bounced off.

The evening grew longer. The demonstrators grew tired. Few complained, but many were curious. They were not getting the usual positive vibrations from Hosea, who looked haggard and weary. Then, suddenly, as if he'd blown in on a fresh breeze, there stood Jesse Jackson, who has been described as being closer than anyone else to Dr. King in charisma and in his acceptance of nonviolence as a way of life. Jackson was wearing a white turtle-neck sweater, and he towered above the crowd. Reaching for the bullhorn, he began, "Brothers and sisters, we got business to take care of." "Sock soul, brother!" "We got a lot of work to do on this thing, and we gonna march now on over to the church where they're having the rally to help take care of this business." Corky looked stunned. Hosea looked relieved. And the crowd of demonstrators obediently lined up and marched away.

The conflict between the causes of the Mexican-Americans and those of the blacks had come to a head. The relationship had been strained all along, but the S.C.L.C. and Tiejerina had kept it going in the interest of unity and solidarity. Tiejerina's lieutenant, Corky Gonzales, had demanded that Hosea support the demonstration at the Justice Department, and really didn't seem interested in much else. Hosea didn't mind being arrested. In fact, he wanted to be arrested. But this cause—the release in California of a small group of Mexican-Americans charged with conspiracy—just didn't seem broad enough. Corky thought otherwise.

Jackson was not only fresher than Hosea that night— not having been on the demonstration in the hot sun all day—but he was better equipped to deal with Corky, whose orientation was closer to that of the urban hustlers

Jesse Jackson was used to dealing with.

The around-the-clock demonstrations at the Agriculture Department were perhaps the most strenuous ordeals for the demonstrators. More people than usual were asleep during the day at R.C. because they had been up all night sitting on the steps of the Department. And they remained there, regardless of the weather.

One morning, as a weary group stood waiting to be replaced, the sky grew gray and a slight cool wind began to blow. As a heavy downpour of cold rain began, most of the group huddled together under army blankets and started singing.

The last demonstration I attended was on Solidarity Day. In that great mass of 50,000 or more people, I looked for the faces that I had come to know over the last few weeks. I saw only a few, and concluded that the veteran residents of R.C. just happened to be in places that I was not. Later, as the program dragged on and I became weary from the heat, I walked back into the city, expecting to find it empty. Instead I saw the people I had been looking for outside. J.T. and Leon and many others.

Harry Jackson, a cabinet-maker from Baltimore, sat in his usual place—inside the fenced-in compound of the Baltimore delegation. He was keeping watch over the two dormitories—women to the left, men to the right—and a frying pan of baked beans cooking on a small, portable grill. Since he was not out demonstrating, I asked him why he had come to R.C. in the first place. "We came because of the lack of association between the black man and the white man. If the system don't integrate itself, it will segregate itself all over again. Our group was integrated. We had one white fellow from the University of Massachussetts. But he hasn't been back."

This man, I thought, was probably typical of the majority of R.C. residents. They wanted things to get better, and felt that they would if people got together. The system didn't have to come down; it just needed overhauling. Still, the system had created the provincialism and distrust of larger communities that prompted Harry Jackson to remark as I was leaving, "I believe we should keep the people together who came together."

As I walked through Resurrection City, in the distance I could hear the sound of voices coming from the Lincoln Memorial—voices too distant to be understood. After a while, I ran across Leon and J.T. Leon said he was on the way to his A-frame.

"Why aren't you out at the demonstration?" I asked. And barely able to keep his eyes open, he replied weakly, "My demonstration was all night last night. Up at the Agriculture Department. And I'll be there again, all night tonight. That's why I've just got to get some sleep."

A few days later, Jackson and Leon and J.T. and every other resident of Resurrection City were either arrested (for civil disobedience) or tear-gassed (for convenience) by policemen from the District of Columbia. The structures came down in less than half the time it took to put them up. And Resurrection City was dead. Up on the hill, spokesmen for S.C.L.C. said they had achieved some of the goals of the campaign and were making progress toward achieving more. But the people were all—or mostly all—gone.

So, in the end, what did Resurrection City do? It certainly made the poor visible. But did it make them effective? Mr. Abernathy would have them believe that it did. And the people who believed him were, by and large, the ones who had come out of the same area that he had come from. An observer once said that Mr. Abernathy lived for the few hours when he could escape back to his church in Atlanta for Sunday services. This was home. Those who came out of that background were the ones who would have stayed in Washington until their leader said the job was done, working diligently all the while. But they, too, would be glad to get back home.

The confrontations of rural Negroes, not only with officials and the police but with urban blacks as well, may have engendered in them a bit of cynicism—perhaps even a bit of militancy. But one suspects that the talk, for years to come, will be of how they went to Washington and, for all practical purposes, "stood on Eastland's toes."

For the urban-rural types, who were in a transitional position to begin with, the frustrations inherent in the system became only more apparent. Already leaning toward urban-type militancy, their inclinations were reenforced by the treatment that even the nonviolent received when those in control grew weary of them and their cause.

The urban people did not learn anything that they hadn't already known. Except, perhaps, about the differences that exist between them and their Southern brothers. They expected nothing, they gave little, and they got the same in return.

Resurrection City was not really supposed to succeed as a city. It was supposed to succeed in dramatizing the plight of the poor in this country. Instead, its greatest success was in dramatizing what the system has done to the black community in this country. And in doing so, it affirmed the view taken by black militants today—that before black people can make any meaningful progress in the United States of America, they have to, as the militants say, "get themselves together."

October 1968

Poverty Programs And Policy Priorities

MARTIN REIN/S. M. MILLER

The war on poverty is financially boxed in—on the one side, by the military priorities for the war in Vietnam, and on the other, by conservative domestic politics and assaults. In this state of siege, its progress is limited. But even if the conflict in Vietnam—and in Congress—were to end tomorrow, the anti-poverty program would still face major battles and possible defeat. For success in any program depends on strategy as well as resources. Given vastly greater funds and lowered political opposition, basic questions would still have to be answered: Which projects should the government support? How well are they planned? What can they realistically accomplish? What goals come first?

It is not the purpose of this article to recommend specific programs, whether old or new, which should be continued or started. Rather, we are concerned with helping to construct a workable framework for making such decisions—a framework needed under any circumstances of war or peace.

To set up priorities, we must consider what is wanted (values), what could be effective (rationality), and what is politically and organizationally *feasible*. We must not only know what benefits we seek, and why, but what we are willing to pay, or give up, to achieve them. Goals very often conflict; to promote one may not only mean neglecting others, but even working against them. Values must not be buried under technical considerations—the "whys" lost sight of because of the "hows." The kind of nation and life we think worthwhile—our view of the good society—must help determine the programs we choose.

There are no final or absolute answers here. Rather, let us explore what choices are available, how people choose, and how they should go about choosing.

Most programs for reducing poverty to date, whether in the planning or implementation stage, fall under six major headings: amenities, investing in human capital, transfers, rehabilitation, participation, economic measures.

■ AMENITIES. These are concerned with supplying services that strengthen and enrich the quality of life, that directly modify the environment of the poor. They serve as increments to personal and family welfare, whether as household help, child care facilities, or information centers. They extend the quality of living; if the poor have them, they are less poor in the sense of being without services. Alfred Kahn calls them "social utilities" and considers them as necessary as such public utilities as water and roads. They should not be considered remedies for a disease, but a normal and accepted service.

■ INVESTING IN HUMAN CAPITAL. Investment of wealth is a means of creating more wealth. Investments in "human capital" (an in-term among economists) concentrate resources on making the poor more self-sufficient and productive: schooling, job training, health care, and various techniques of fitting them into the job market. Theodore W. Schultz believes that "changes in the investment in human capital" are the basic and most effective means for "reducing the inequality . . . of personal income," rather than such devices as progressive taxes.

But what is a good investment? The purposes of "investments in human capital" are not as clear-cut as the parallel with investment in physical capital implies. What purposes, for instance, are educational programs in the war on poverty designed to accomplish? There is considerable confusion about this. In the nineteenth century, the emphasis in the charity schools was on inculcating character—good work habits and such traits as industry, promptness, and reliability—rather than in teaching the specific skills and abilities necessary to rise in the world. The Job Corps and Neighborhood Youth Programs frequently seem intent on following this nineteenth-century model. The rhetoric of these programs implies that the goal is increasing lifetime earnings rather than conformity. On the other hand, "good character" seems to be a prerequisite for higher salaries.

■ TRANSFERS. Transfers provide cash to the poor (and to other groups in society). Devices include the proposed negative income tax, fatherlessness insurance, children's allowances, guaranteed income, and various cash subsidies. They are a means of redistributing income outside the market place. Cash transfers to the poor could be provided in a way that promotes self-respect and perpetuates the myth that they, like the farmer or subsidized industry, are actually helping the country by accepting the money. Transfers emphasize a way to build up and assure total income, instead of the 1930's emphasis on replacing income lost because of illness, unemployment, accident, or old age.

But American public policy has been biased against the use of transfer payments to reduce poverty. We seem continually haunted by that legacy of Victorianism that a guaranteed income (for the poor) must increase shiftlessness, immorality, and illegitimacy. Subsidy payments to farmers or industry rouse few doubts about the danger to the moral fiber of their recipients. Public assistance programs seem less concerned with whether the poor get enough as the harm it might do them if they did. The prevailing orthodoxy (see Title V of the Economic Opportunity Act and the 1962 amendments to the Social Security Act) is committed to change sources of income rather than to increase it, to "get people off the dole"—Title V by work training and the amendments by social services.

■ REHABILITATION. This approach concentrates on changing people, usually by psychological means, to restore social functioning. It ranges from guidance and counseling, through casework, to psychotherapy and psychoanalysis. Rehabilitation hopes to overcome poverty by overcoming personal and family disorganization and deviancy. Those reclaimed will become more acceptable, more employable, more competent. Rehabilitation, seeking to change the person, accepts the environment as it is.

■ PARTICIPATION. Participation includes those activities that try to overcome many of the psychological and social effects of poverty by giving the poor a stake in society and a chance to affect their own destinies. As Alan Haber says:

American poverty, while it involves considerable physical hardship, is primarily "social poverty." It isolates the individual from the social mainstream, denies him the respect and status of the "respectable" members of the society, and excludes him from mobility opportunities into positions of social worth.

But there seems a confusion of purpose. Is the primary goal and effect of this strategy to help the poor to help themselves, or is it a means to organize them so that they can exert collective power? Warren G. Haggstrom has emphasized the more common concern with participation as a psychological condition of powerlessness. Involvement "provides immediate and compelling psychological returns." But another interpretation comes from Richard A. Cloward: "Economic deprivation is fundamentally a political problem, and power will be required to solve it."

■ ECONOMIC MEASURES. One economic approach to reducing poverty uses the "dribble-down" concept—if production is stimulated and the nation prospers at the top, some of the benefits will also dribble down to the poor. Another approach favors "bubbling up" the poor into the economic mainstream by programs designed directly to benefit them—new jobs, more low-skill jobs, minimum wages, and so on. Which is the best way to promote economic growth and full employment? Some economists emphasize selective training for those jobs that are still unfilled and creation of special new job opportunities (for instance, nonprofessionals' in hospitals and agencies). Others believe that the economy as a whole should be heated up so that a near-full employment situation emerges. But the concern with price increases, loosely called inflation, tends to stymie high-level employment, and many of the poor are low-skilled and not likely to be employed except with special inducements to employers.

To sum up, the six intervention strategies can be conceived of as attempts to change environment (amenities) ; to change occupational chances (investment) ; to change the pattern of claims on income distributed outside the market (transfers) ; to change people (rehabilitation) ; to change the distribution of power (participation) ; and, finally, to change the performance of the economic system (economic measures).

This inventory outlines not only a list of policy choices, but also embodies different conceptions about the meaning and causes of poverty. The different definitions of poverty imply different means to overcome it. What appears to be a concern with "poverty" is actually a tissue of sometimes conflicting agenda. The term "poverty" cloaks the competing objectives. We note six ways to describe poverty, beyond mere lack of money:

■ POVERTY AND SOCIAL DECENCY. By this conception, citizens have a right not only to freedom from want, which requires a minimum of income, but also to adequate (and not inexpensive) services. One cannot reduce poverty without providing housing, medical care, and recreation. The lack of these amenities is then, by definition, poverty.

■ POVERTY AND EQUALITY. Proponents of this view hold that poverty exists as long as the botton fifth (or tenth) of the population receives a shrinking or stable share of a growing economic pie. Their concern is with inequality—the position of lowest income groups *relative* to the rest of the nation. Improving the absolute level of a group without decreasing the gap between it and other groups may heighten its sense of relative deprivation. Improvement in absolute standards can lead to frustration and discontent, as the case of the Negro in the United States illustrates. Reducing poverty requires reducing inequality.

The goal of equity is not simply a matter of taking from the rich to give to the poor, but requires a searching way of examining the distribution of government largesse. For example, in housing we lump tax concessions with public housing expenditures as forms of government subsidy (as Richard Titmuss suggests), then we reach the startling conclusion that the major beneficiaries of housing welfare policies are the middle and upper classes. Alvin Schorr estimates that subsidies to the upper income fifth in 1962 were twice those to the bottom fifth ($1.7 billion to $820 million). Good housing therefore becomes simply a matter of equal treatment—the poor should receive at least as much from the government as the rich.

■ POVERTY AND MOBILITY. Poverty, according to this conception, is the lack of opportunity to alter one's income, occupational, or social position. In a rigidly stratified social structure, those at the bottom, even if above a subsistence level, are still poor: They cannot escape upward. Enlisted men in the armed forces are not in want, and they may receive amenities as a matter of right; but they may be, as William Grigsby has pointed out, nevertheless in poverty if they are forced to remain in a rigid social niche. Similarly the Negro—stuck at the bottom of the social hierarchy—must be considered poor even if he has an adequate livelihood. Whether or not children remain in the same social and occupational classes as their parents, therefore, can be used as a measure of the reduction of poverty and the rigidity of the social order.

■ POVERTY AND SOCIAL CONTROL. For many, improved income and services cannot be enough—for they are concerned with the social problems associated with poverty: alcoholism, delinquency, illiteracy, illegitimacy, mental illness. In the rhetoric of professionals, rehabilitation contributes to "self-actualization," but in fact it is more often used for social control—getting the poor to behave according to accepted standards. This view frequently merges into a broader concern with social harmony and equilibrium. If reducing poverty among Negroes did not eliminate race riots, the programs would be considered failures.

■ POVERTY AND SOCIAL INCLUSION. In this view, people are poor when they cannot participate in the major institutions of our society, particularly the institutions that affect their lives—that is, when they have little or nothing to say about schools, employment, law enforcement, or even welfare and other social services. "The meaning of poverty," writes Peter Marris, "is humiliation: lack of power, of dignity, of self respect. . . . It is a mark of inferiority, and so more damaging than want itself."

Some experts justify reducing poverty for economic reasons—the poor will spend their increased incomes for necessities and comforts and improve the economy; if the money went instead to the middle class, more would simply go into savings. Therefore, as the poor prosper, all will prosper. Humanitarian and economic goals coalesce.

But what if they should come to conflict? Then, to follow this concept to its logical conclusion, economic considerations must be given priority. We must prevent inflation even at the cost of preserving, or increasing, poverty; economic growth is more important than redistribution. At these points, the concern with the economy sharply displaces the interest in helping the poor or reducing poverty.

These different concepts lead us to at least three basic models of how to view the overall purposes of social policy:

■ ALLOCATIVE JUSTICE. Policy is guided by a commitment to the more equitable distribution of benefits—who gets what, where, why and how. This model emphasizes equal opportunity for investment in career jobs and education and for the redistribution of amenities, income, and resources necessary for well being.

■ POLICY AS HANDMAIDEN. This strategy seeks to promote programs that reduce poverty, but these are subordinate to other goals, such as economic growth, social stability, or physical renewal of cities. Thus, transfer payments to the poor could be primarily supported because they stimulate the economy. Or services and amenities to the poor could be aimed at reducing social unrest, providing a silent strategy for riot control. Or the major purpose of rehabilitation of the poor in slums could be to make them good tenants and to facilitate the relocation of those displaced by urban renewal programs aimed at increasing the real estate values of downtown areas. These programs are designed to win the joint support of what might otherwise be competing groups. But in case of conflict the secondary role of poverty policy becomes evident.

■ POLICY AS THERAPY. Many people, including a disproportionate number of the poor, do not behave according to our prevailing, accepted, and predominantly middle class standards. Poverty programs may exact conformity. Rehabilitation programs illustrate this approach.

This analysis leads to four fundamental policy questions. What are the purposes of the programs? How effective are they in achieving them? How feasible are they politically (what are the chances of getting them adopted and implemented)? How do we choose between competing desirable programs or goals?

The question of purpose involves much more than technical classifications. It includes value judgments about goals. For instance, do we consider adequate housing and health programs for the poor *amenities* (to make the quality of their lives more comfortable) or *investments* (good housing to prevent poverty, and good health to reduce unemployment and improve learning in school)?

It is a political question as well: Will legislators vote funds for an anti-poverty program unless we contend it will reduce poverty and crime or welfare costs? But a technical and rational question also is involved: What is the evidence that better housing and medical care will prevent poverty? Can we document the charge that the poor are really the most victimized by these insufficiencies?

Alvin Schorr has made an impressive and persuasive attempt to bring together evidence on the relationship between housing and poverty. He concludes:

The following effects may spring from poor housing: A perception of one's self that leads to pessimism and passivity, stress to which the individual cannot adapt, poor health, and a state of dissatisfaction; pleasure in company but not in solitude, cynicism about people and organizations, a high degree of sexual stimulation without legitimate outlet, and difficulty in household management and child rearing; and relationships that tend to spread out in the neighborhood rather than deeply into the family.

He believes that malnutrition, poor health, and inadequate housing reinforce each other in causing, and intensifying, poverty. As he sees it, it is not the "life styles" of the poor that disable them so much as the lack of means to live properly. What they need is not psychological or sociological analysis but health, housing, adequate incomes.

Others disagree. Their studies indicate to them that improved housing has little effect on such things as deviant behavior or physical illness. Nathan Glazer, for instance, challenges Schorr's assumption:

The chief problems of our slums are social—unemployment, poor education, broken families, crime. . . . Nor can they be solved by physical means, whether by urban renewal projects or . . . housing directly for the poor.

In fact, Glazer believes that social relationships have more effect on housing than vice versa; that broken families can nullify the effects of even the best housing. The facts Glazer quotes are impressive: Two-thirds of the poorest urban families (under $2,000 a year) do not live in substandard housing; further, most of substandard housing is not occupied by the poorest.

What about the traditional relationship between morbidity and poverty? Charles Kadushin concludes: "A review of the evidence . . . leads to the conclusion that . . . there is very little association between getting a disease and social class, although the lower class still feel sicker." That is, Kadushin says, the poor complain more about illness and stay away from work longer for it, but are not necessarily more ill.

Others challenge Kadushin's interpretation. Further, these data do not provide an argument against the development of health and housing programs for poor people. If health and housing seem unrelated, this may be because of difficult problems of measurement. Are the poor who live in standard housing overcrowded? Do they pay too high a portion of their income for this housing? They may be largely older people living in their own homes, while the families with many children live in substandard apartments. Inadequate statistics can distort the total picture.

Let us consider health in the same light. Even if morbidity rates among the poor are low, infant mortality is high, life is shorter, hospitalization longer, and disability has more severe consequences.

The fact is that we have so little good policy-oriented research that we cannot make any firm conclusion about the relationships between poverty and housing and health care. Consequently, we cannot be sure that better housing and health would help raise the poor from poverty.

But housing and health can be justified on other grounds than reducing poverty. Equality, as noted, is one. Inequalities and loss of dignity might be the crucial aspects of poor housing. According to Schorr: "It makes little difference whether bad housing is a result or a cause of poverty, it is an integral part of being poor." And the psychology of poverty is reinforced by seeing, all about, how the other half lives. By this definition, then, people without adequate housing or access to medical care are poor; adequate amenities reduce poverty. It is not that housing is instrumental to improved education or income; it is a goal in itself.

The second policy issue is effectiveness. What good is a program that does not accomplish its purpose? But, in the first place, what is a program's purpose? Anyone who tries to get a straightforward statement of goals from a social agency usually finds that they react as though their very reason for being were under challenge.

But if the agencies will not provide clear answers, what of social science itself? For instance, do present rehabilitation programs actually reduce deviancy? When the score is finally totaled, the answer turns out to be, mostly, no. Social science research generally winds up exploding myths rather than giving solutions. William Kvaracecous, who recently reviewed the literature on delinquency, has reached the gloomy conclusion that nothing works very well. Other studies support him. Social work techniques may make youths and groups more democratic, more willing to join in approved sports and dancing, but they have little effect on law-breaking. Walter Miller has concluded that delinquency depends largely on age and sex—young men commit most crimes—and therapy will not change these conditions.

Will rehabilitation and counseling help broken or ineffective families or reduce economic dependency? A number of studies—including the most recent analysis of a vocational high school by Henry Meyer—and his associates—indicate that intensive casework makes little difference in reducing social problems.

However, ineffectiveness alone is not always enough reason to abandon a strategy. A program can be effective in unplanned ways. Even if rehabilitation does not reduce pathology and poverty much, its ethical, moral, and humanitarian value should not be discounted.

Another practical political factor impedes effectiveness: We frequently adopt programs not because of demonstrated validity, but because they are feasible—we can get them adopted and financially supported. "It is always easier to put up a clinic than tear down a slum," Barbara Wootton argues. "We prefer today to analyze the infected individual rather than the infection from the environment." Rehabilitation as a means of reducing dependency has become a national policy. Also, for political reasons we have reversed the usual procedure by starting programs and *then* testing the concepts in demonstration projects. In such situations the pressure to find exactly the answers we are already committed to is hard to resist. Thus, what is politically possible makes a rational analysis difficult.

What of the argument that the poor should, as a policy, be encouraged to achieve power through collective action and pressure? Alvin Schorr has summarized the arguments against such grassroots involvement:

> Efforts to promote self-organization fail more often than they succeed. . . . First, poor people have learned cynicism from bitter experience. They do not widely and readily respond to efforts to organize them. Second, when they do seek serious ends for themselves, they threaten established institutions or interest groups. At that point they are likely to learn once more that they are comparatively powerless. Third, the professionals who try to help them have, with rare exceptions, one foot in the "establishment." The ethical and practical problems that arise in their marginal situation are not solved simply by an effort of will.

The foregoing leads us to the third policy issue—the feasibility of programs that invest in human resource de-

velopment. If we say that investment in education or training will result in jobs, can we deliver? Is there a coherent
relationship between the learning and the job?

More education or training usually pays off in more and
better employment. But how much education—and expense
—before the payoff starts? College graduates are better off
than others, and the income differences between them and
the non-college population are expanding. But the differences in job opportunities and wages between high school
graduates and dropouts are not great, especially for non-
whites. They seem, in fact, to be declining. For males
age 35 to 44 in 1939, dropouts earned 80 percent as much
as high school graduates; in 1961, 87 percent. As more
people get more education, the tipping point for education
may come later and later. Investing in human resources
may have a limited gain if would-be dropouts do not go
to college.

How much education, how good, and how relevant to
the job market are all important questions in job training.
And on one or more of these counts most of our training
programs have fallen down. A study of "successful" ex-
convicts shows that only 17 percent were working at the
trades they had learned in prison. Of 1,700 young people
who applied to Mobilization for Youth for training, only
"roughly one in four eventually achieved competitive employment as a direct result . . . ," according to Richard A.
Cloward. And these were mostly for marginal jobs, paying
marginal salaries. As Herbert E. Klarman says: ". . . in
the past the market economy has apparently not absorbed
appreciable numbers of rehabilitated persons."

The relationship between occupational training and unemployment is very low. First, whatever its faults, we have
done a much better job of rehabilitating people than of
preparing society to receive them; and training means little

if it does not lead to jobs. The connection between jobs and training is frequently very loose. Second, our training programs are often simply not good or relevant enough. Cloward reveals that the youths who did graduate from the MFY program could not read better than when they started, and had failed to get skills that could qualify them for the higher pay jobs. Training just to improve character or work habits—the intent of many if not most training programs for low-income youth—is a poor investment.

Moreover, employers tend not to take this training seriously, or consider it a legitimate "credential" of employability. One of the great virtues of a diploma, or even an honorable military discharge, is that an employer will recognize it as a "credential" of employability and character.

Why train if that training is inadequate, discounted, or if no jobs are available? Real improvement can only come about with changes in our educational, referral, and economic institutions—which are untouched by the training programs. In short, unless relevant institutions themselves are changed, even highly promising programs will be frustrating rather than improving prospects. Training can be an effort to evade the issue of job availability.

Few people will argue that better training and more jobs for the poor are not desirable goals. But the stubborn facts are that most training is not good enough, and that the jobs which follow training are too often marginal or scarce. Education, to yield large payoffs, will need large investments. Are we willing to face these difficulties?

What happens when goals conflict, whether the conflict is real or apparent, recognized or ignored?

As Isaiah Berlin has astutely observed, there is a "natural tendency of all but a few thinkers to believe that all the things they hold good must be intimately connected or at least compatible with one another." In social policy, as in other fields, this is a delusion; goals often conflict, and we must decide on priorities. Here are four major areas of real or assumed value conflict:

■ PRICES AND POVERTY. Paul Samuelson and Robert Solow have concluded that a 5.5 percent level of unemployment is necessary to keep prices stable; anything less must result in inflation. "It may be doubted . . . that we can achieve both a satisfactory level of employment and price stability without major improvements in our antiinflationary weapons." Similarly, the British Labor government has recently discovered, with some distress, that if it strengthens its international economic position, it may have to let unemployment rise and renege on its promise to raise pensions.

In short, we may have to choose between social welfare programs and rising prices. As James Tobin says:

> We are paying much too high a social price for avoiding creeping inflation and for protecting our gold supply and "the dollar." . . . The interests of the unemployed, the poor and the Negroes are underrepresented in the consensus which supports and confines current policy.

■ INCOME PLANS AND INCENTIVES. Raising incomes through payments can conflict with trying to get the poor into the labor market. Is providing an incentive to work more important than assuring adequacy of income? As Evelyn Burns puts it:

> Workers whose normal incomes are very low and whose economic horizons are very limited may, if social security income is adequate for their modest wants, prefer benefit status to securing an income from employment, particularly if their normal type of employment is arduous or unpleasant, or if they are unmarried with no family responsibilities.

■ RIGHTS AND MISUSE. Support programs contain various

tests of eligibility, and provisions to punish violators. These are supposed to prevent cheating and make sure that welfare does not interfere with the free labor market and private economic incentives. These goals, however, conflict with those of economic costs and social rights. Obviously, the greater the gap between benefits and wages, the less effectively welfare can serve to increase demands in time of recession, and generally stabilize the economy; and the more rigid the rules and administrative control over welfare payments, the less chance of reducing feelings of powerlessness among the poor, and of establishing social benefits as legal *rights*.

■ ORDER AND CONFLICT. The goals of keeping public order and protecting the well-to-do and of safeguarding the social and constitutional rights of the poor often conflict. We have not only a law about the poor, which seeks to deal with their condition, but a law *of* the poor, based on police powers. As Jacobus Ten Broek has declared, it is "designed to safeguard health, safety, morals, and well-being of the fortunate rather than directly to improve the lot of the unfortunate." The goal is the protection of society against the poor rather than safeguarding the poor from an indifferent or callous society. When we encourage the poor to be militant and independent, to secure and exercise the legal rights to assistance and protection, we tend to sharpen this conflict. If they are to try to shape policy, they may become involved in boycotts, pickets, strikes, and other dramatic forms of protest—in other words, in threatening the "well-being of the fortunate." In such areas as school desegregation, the interests of the fortunate will be directly pitted against those of the unfortunate. These are natural conflicts in a pluralistic society.

Thus, the single, seemingly simple aim of reducing poverty hides the many and often contradictory goals deriving from different conceptions of what poverty is. They call for many different kinds of strategy, which cannot hope to satisfy everybody.

How do we establish rules to allocate limited resources to promote goals that are in partial conflict? Can we develop more effective methods of making decisions that specifically recognize contrasting objectives and give policy-makers a clearer choice of the costs and benefits of various combinations?

Cost-benefit analysis has become more popular as older decision-making methods have proven inadequate for fighting poverty. The economic market had long been the traditional way of making decisions—automatic, impersonal. More recently, politicians and their administrators have made many important decisions—reflecting the play of political and value preferences. But though it moderated some of the dangers of market decisions, political determination has brought new strains of its own—arbitrariness, and the obscuring of national needs because of political traditions and expediency. Cost-benefit analysis seeks to professionalize decision-making. It offers a rational, as opposed to a market or political (value) basis for making decisions. Means are in agreement with goals.

It makes important contributions. But it does not provide a mechanism for superseding questions of value and preference. When used that way, it has important defects. Our criticism of cost-benefit analysis is six-fold: It suffers from technical limitations; it can lead to a quantitative mentality; the issue of operational feasibility is largely ignored; it has no ready-made response to the basic question of what costs and which benefits; goals are difficult to delineate; and it does not deal with the issue of competing goals. The large-scale danger in cost-benefit analysis is that values surreptitiously and inevitably creep in. The covert handling of values limits democratic discussions. Nor does it, we believe, strengthen in the long-run an effective policy of poverty or inequality-reduction.

It implies knowledge and confidence about social data that are ill placed. One does not have to agree with the doubts that we have raised in this paper about the efficacy of housing or the connection between health and poverty to doubt that one can have much confidence in measurements of costs and benefits. Hunches are frequently more important than scientific determination. Obviously social science will develop and some uncertainties will diminish. But we cannot be confident that all our evaluations are based upon scientific proof and that in the future we will always have a firm scientific basis for choices to be faced.

Another technical problem is the question of the "interest rate." In order to calculate cost and benefits which are received or expended over a number of years, it is necessary to use some way to calculate future benefits in terms of their present value. Since present gains are valued more than future, the latter should be reduced by an appropriate discount. The level of the discount can markedly affect total benefits. For example, cost-benefit analysis of much vocational education would have different results if a higher discount rate were employed than in some present calculations. The appropriate level of the discount is not undebatable.

The result of looking at benefits over a long number of years is, therefore, inevitably an emphasis on youth. The longer individuals can benefit from a program, the greater the return. It pays then to concentrate on youth rather than on the aged. But are there not other reasons for concentrating on older workers?

Cost-benefit analysis tends to emphasize those variables that can be reduced to figures. For example, the inability in urban renewal to assign a monetary value to the aesthetic pleasure of greenery may be a serious difficulty. There is danger of sliding into the position that the only goals with merit and legitimacy are those that are quantifiable and convertible into money. Quantitative reasoning may lead to stressing productivity (return per unit of expenditure) over total results. Productivity can be high while total returns may be less than in some other kind of activity which has a high relative cost per unit of expenditure. For instance, it may be more "productive" to work with the highly educated, "cream" unemployed because it is easier to get them jobs than it is for the hard-core, long-term unemployed individuals. But which activity comes closer to solving the problems of unemployment?

Quantitative reasoning also tends to underestimate the importance of feasibility. Here we do not refer to the political issues, but to the effective implementation of a program. It may be that a particular program is highly productive with a likelihood of a return far outweighing its cost. But this program may be extremely difficult to mount because of manpower or administrative obstacles. Another program may have a much poorer prospect in terms of productivity and costs, but be much easier to implement.

In making these points, we do not argue that the defects cannot be remedied, rather that current practice tends to ignore them. But now we move into issues which are more basic to the long-term difficulties of cost-benefit analysis.

What is a cost and what is a benefit is not so obvious as it seems. To a large extent cost-benefit analysis narrows the definition of both cost and benefit. To what extent are second and third order effects of any action included in the analysis? This is largely a political and value question more than a technical one.

What is the goal? Our foregoing analysis has stressed

competing goals. Which should have priority is not only a question of rational calculations but of political issues and value preferences. Cost-benefit analysis provides some important kinds of information, but it does not resolve the issues of values, direction, purposes, or priorities. Is the goal to bring the poor up to a certain income level? Or is it a larger one of reducing inequalities within society?

Which is preferable cannot be determined by cost-benefit analysis alone. Cost-benefit analysis at best is only a tool. It may be useful, but it also can be misleading when assumed to have greater clarifying power than it actually has.

We must not be lulled into thinking that cost-benefit analysis can rescue us from choice. Three solutions—cost-benefit analysis, the marketplace, the political process—are probably necessary, but none is sufficient alone, or even together. Policy is not all about technical rules for implementing value-neutral hardware. No simple choices are on hand. The crucial issues remain: How do we define a good society? How do we implement it?

These questions must be confronted. Technology must serve purpose. There are several ways to reveal the techniques of policy-making as the politics that they are. One good way may be to create a pluralistic system of advisory planning where many interest groups have their own experts to develop and support their own policies. Herbert Gans suggests that this may have already developed in city planning, where a progressive wing concentrates on social planning and a conservative wing defends "traditional physical planning and . . . middle class values."

Value judgments have to be made—but who, specifically, shall make them? However it is done—overtly or covertly, consciously or unconsciously, democratically or dictatorially —it occurs. The planner is not a value-free technician serving a value-free bureaucracy. The assumption that politics is without content—only efficient or inefficient—is unacceptable. As Paul Davidoff says: "Appropriate policy in a democracy is determined through a political debate. The right course of action is always a matter of choice, never a fact." The search for "rationality" cannot avoid the issues of objectives and ideologies.

There should be many analyses, based on competing outlooks as well as assumptions. In a pluralistic, competitive society the people should weigh competing values, vigorously promoted, before they can make just decisions. But ultimately, after all technical analyses are made, the selection of goals and timing must depend on judgment; and judgment must depend on those brute preferences we call values.

September 1967

Reporting
on the
Social State of the Union

WALTER F. MONDALE

America's social goals were well stated by the writers of the Constitution: to "establish justice, insure domestic tranquility, provide for the common defense, promote the general welfare, and secure the blessings of liberty for ourselves and our posterity." But in 1968 we see little domestic tranquility; we see little justice for a substantial number of citizens; and for millions—poorly educated, ill-housed, or otherwise deprived—the blessings of liberty are a cruel jest.

The search for solutions to this modern dilemma leads those of us in government to turn to social research. There is increasing legislative hunger for social-science counsel. Senator Abraham Ribicoff, in major hearings on the urban crises, called no fewer than 12 social scientists to testify. In order to improve the federal government's social-science research capability, Senator Fred Harris of Oklahoma has reintroduced legislation to establish a national foundation for the social sciences. He seeks to draw the

107

social sciences from the shadow of the National Science Foundation, thus giving them independent status and increased stature.

In government departments, a new kind of administrator is emerging. For example, Daniel P. Moynihan, former Assistant Secretary of Labor, is "one of a new breed of public servants, the social-scientist-politicos, who combine in their backgrounds both social-science training and full-time involvement in political activity." (See Black Families and the White House," Lee Rainwater and William L. Yancey, *Trans*-action July/August 1966.) Another new political animal in federal departments and agencies is the systems-approach expert, who—by means of cost-effectiveness analysis and other tools—seeks to help decision-makers understand all relevant alternatives and key interaction among them by calculating costs, risks, and potential results associated with each course of action. An example of this new breed is William Gorham, formerly of the Pentagon and the RAND Corporation, and Assistant Secretary for Planning and Evaluation at the Department of Health, Education, and Welfare, who has been appointed head of the Urban Institute, a government-supported independent research center.

The development of these new types of scientist-politicians suggests a governmental institution—an arm of the executive—that can combine a knowledge of sociology, science, history, social psychology, criminology, and social economics. These new specialists can place their knowledge in a governmental context, and bring a systems approach to bear on broad social programs.

Early last year I introduced in the Senate the Full Opportunity and Social Accounting Act, which was cosponsored by Senators Clark, Hart, Harris, Inouye, Kennedy of Massachusetts, McCarthy, McGee, Muskie, Nelson, and

Proxmire, who is chairman of the Joint Economic Committee. This legislation would draw the social scientists into the inner councils of the Administration; it would foster the use of the systems approach for an overview of the broad range of domestic social programs; and it would establish a system of social accounting to keep a constant check on our domestic social status. Furthermore, it would require a public report of this social audit.

In its statement of policy, the Full Opportunity and Social Accounting Act reaffirms that "it is the continuing policy and responsibility of the federal government, consistent with the primary responsibilities of the state and local government and the private sector, to promote and encourage such conditions as will give every American the opportunity to live in decency and dignity, and to provide a clear and precise picture of whether such conditions are promoted and encouraged in such areas as health, education and training, rehabilitation, housing, vocational opportunities, the arts and humanities, and special assistance for the deprived, the abandoned, and the criminal."

To accomplish this, the legislation would:

—declare social accounting a national goal;

—establish the President's Council of Social Advisers, comparable in the social sphere to the Council of Economic Advisers in the economic area;

—require the President to submit an annual Social Report to Congress, the social counterpart to his Economic Report; and

—create a joint committee of Congress to examine the substance of the Social Report.

In his Social Report, the President is to detail "the overall progress and effectiveness of federal efforts" toward implementing the policy of the act; review state, local, and private efforts to this end; and present "current and foreseeable needs, programs, and policies and recommendations for legislation."

The three-member Council of Social Advisers, supported by a staff of experts in the social sciences and in those natural sciences concerned with man and his environment, would be empowered to "gather timely and authoritative information and statistical data" and analyze and interpret them. The Council would also appraise the various programs and activities of the federal government and develop priorities for the programs, recommending to the President the most efficient and effective way to allocate federal resources.

The model for this act is the Employment Act of 1946, which has had an indisputably favorable effect on the nation's economy. This economic progress—owing in large part to highly refined economic analysis and indicators— is a powerful argument for using social analysis and measurement.

The Council of Economic Advisers recommends measures to maintain a stable, prosperous, and expanding economy. It operates on four assumptions:
—that welfare (the ultimate objective) is dependent upon the level and health of national economic activity;
—that economic factors can be quantified;
—that action by government can cause specific changes in the national economic condition; and
—that from analysis of economic data it is feasible to recommend specific action to achieve national economic health.

To do its job, the C.E.A. had to develop a system of economic criteria to measure the present and prospective conditions of the economy. It had to increase the expertise and the rigor of the economics discipline in order to reduce the margin of error in economic measurement. It had to develop tools of economic analysis, calling upon the entire community of economists for contributions. It had to proceed with caution so as to command the respect and acceptance of decision-makers. Finally, its recommendations and findings had to be action-oriented.

The same process is now appropriate and necessary in the social endeavors of the federal government. But we should mislead no one: This new job will be far more difficult. There should be no false hopes for instant success. For the most part, economic indicators are hard, cash-register data, and in most indices the dollar is available as a uniform measuring unit. Understandably, it is far easier to count the cash in a workingman's pocket than to measure the quality of his health or education.

A true attempt to apply non-economic measures to the quality of life in America could have a revolutionary impact on government. It might be the first time that government looked at the individual to see what government programs do *to* and *for* him—in other words, to discover the effect, rather than merely to measure the effort, of government programs. For example, we know how many people take advantage of Medicare, but there are no public reports on the quality of this care. The same is true of education, criminal rehabilitation, and much of the poverty effort (although the publication of studies on the effect of Head Start has been a laudable beginning).

At present, our social goals are vague and ill defined. The legislative requirement that the Administration deliver a public social accounting should sharpen the Administration's goals and social planning. This could promote setting long-range goals in, for example, education, health care, and the fight against environmental pollution, and encourage definite periodic progress toward their achievement.

Some argue that this system of progress reports will curb innovation and experimentation. But I think we have little to fear if we use fresh, imaginative ideas. And in fact, the lack of adequate indicators can actually conceal the success of government innovations. Critics of the Job Corps, for example, attack the cost per corpsman, while the Corps' effect on the corpsman's life and potential is ignored.

Some see a danger of the indicators' being manipulated for political ends, or the goals deliberately being set so low that accomplishment will appear spectacular. Of course, our political system is, at every level, vulnerable on this score. But there are checks built into the legislation. It provides for a Joint Congressional Committee empowered to probe deeply into the substance of the Social Report—to examine and criticize the declared goals, to question the philosophy behind the various programs, and to test the adequacy of the indicators . For a demonstration of how effective this legislative tool can be, we need only refer to the transcript of the 1967 hearings of the Joint Committee on the Economic Report chaired by Senator William Proxmire.

There are also other legislative checks on the Administration. The General Accounting Office has won a strong reputation for its auditing of Administration expenditures. Senator Abraham Ribicoff has proposed that this operation be expanded by adding an Office of Legislative Evaluation charged with "evaluating the results of the social and economic programs [Congress] has enacted." The Full Opportunity Act proposes to give the Administration new evaluative and analytical equipment. Certainly Congress should be given comparable legislative tools.

The Administration, with the program-planning-budgeting system directed by the Bureau of the Budget, is already taking limited steps toward improving program evaluation and the determining program priorities. And William Gorham, in his work in the Department of Health, Education, and Welfare, has been coordinating a panel working on a "social state of the nation report." No one can guarantee, however, that it will be a permanent institution of government.

As a matter of practical politics, the passage of legislation requires a constituency. Since most laws grow out of a need that has immediacy and relevance for a sizable part of the population, most proposed legislation has a constituency highly motivated to promote its passage. But where is the constituency of legislation that looks to the future—legislation that will have profound impact, yet is currently difficult to understand and in constant danger of being misinterpreted?

To build such a constituency, we must look to the social scientists themselves. And there are other allies as well. At all levels of government, social-welfare organizations and officials are concerned about the effectiveness of programs ranging from welfare to education, from city planning to health care.

The initial job in building a constituency is to bring the legislation to the attention of those for whom it has inherent interest. I have sent letters to 500 social scientists inviting their comment. Furthermore, editorials in media ranging from the *Minneapolis Star* and *Milwaukee Journal* to specialized newsletters have brought encouraging response.

The second step is persuasion, which in this case means education. Few people in policy-making positions are aware of the concept of social accounting—largely because literature on the subject is confined mostly to the academic journals.

The congressional committee is a useful educational device, particularly as an efficient information conduit to the policy-makers. The Full Opportunity and Social Accounting Act has been referred to the Government Operations Committee, which has sent it to Senator Harris's Subcommittee on Governmental Research. In the summer of 1967 that subcommittee held a unique one-day seminar to explore the ramifications of the proposal. Both that session, and the hearings the subcommittee held later, elicited highly illuminating views from social scientists, present and former government officials, businessmen, and journalists. Above all, the discussions buttressed the need for an institutionalized and on-going review of the state of our nation's social health, at the highest level of government as well as on the community and state levels. In great part the hearings produced more questions than answers, and exposed our ignorance rather than a wealth of information about social processes. But our country is now demanding the answers, and it is essential that we begin asking the right questions.

While the Full Opportunity Act will have a vigorous impact upon government, I believe it will have no less impact on the social sciences. There is every reason to believe that the social sciences—like economics since 1946—will be greatly stimulated by enactment of the legislation. Such legislation may prod many social scientists into devoting increased attention to social problems that have specific relevancy to government. Instead of concentrating solely on research and comment, they will become active participants in policymaking.

Are social scientists up to the task? While most who have written me believe that they are, some are less confident. One social scientist of long experience warned, "The behavioral sciences, in my judgment, are in no real position at this point to give any hard data on social problems or conditions." He added, "There are many promises and pretentions; however, when it comes to delivery, what is usually forthcoming are more requests for further research. ... "

If social scientists have not developed the necessary sophistication to fully participate in policy determination, then they *must*—and very soon. For government at all levels is going to ask them for advice and value judgments. This responsibility is going to be thrust upon them, and I don't think they are going to refuse it.

I am encouraged by the reports sent to me by social scientists who are involved in both the planning and the evaluation phases of future-looking projects. The work of organizations such as Resources for the Future and the Russell Sage Foundation is well known. And, of course, virtually every major university has a center or institute doing extremely ambitious research on social problems. Others, such as the Center for Research on the Utilization of Scientific Knowledge at the University of Michigan, are devoting their activity to ways of using scientific skills in the social as well as in the natural sciences. The book *Social Indicators* (M.I.T. Press, 1966), edited by Raymond Bauer, shows how researchers can frame the important questions and meet the basic requirements for social accounting.

All this suggests that some social scientists want to become activists—to convert their role from that of observer to that of participant.

Today, because much valuable information disappears into the academic journals, many policy-makers remain unaware of its existence. A Council of Social Advisers could probably correct this problem by providing a funnel through which the findings of social-science research would be directed to government.

Of course, government policy-makers shouldn't expect a

full range of sophisticated social indicators to be developed overnight, nor should they expect evaluation and analysis that bear the stamp of certainty rather than theory. Scientific progress doesn't work this way. If I read the history of the Council of Economic Advisers correctly, it took that group many years, and experimentation by several Council chairmen, to evolve a satisfactory role in economic analysis and policy recommendation. This will be even more necessary when we are dealing with elusive social values.

Now, a word of warning: There is a history of mistrust on the part of some members of Congress toward the social sciences. This attitude is based partly on unfamiliarity, partly on poor communications between scientists and policy-makers, and partly on the fact that many Congressmen regard themselves as successful practitioners of applied social science—because they have won elections. Institutionalized channels of communication will help break down this mistrust.

Also important is the fact that policy-makers are wary of the political backlash contained in the findings of the social scientists. One dramatic example was the response of policy-makers to the Moynihan Report on the Negro family.

Finally, there are still a substantial number of people who see behavioral-science study as a trend toward the society of Orwell's *1984*. They are wary of invasion of privacy in social research, and fear that data banks will make the individual increasingly vulnerable. These are legitimate concerns, often deeply felt by the social scientists themselves. These concerns demand vigilance. There must be guarantees against misuse of some of the most valuable equipment in social-science research.

But despite these difficulties, it is time to establish an alliance between policy-makers and social scientists. The alliance promises better lives and more individual opportunity through a more orderly approach to the future.

Of this need, former Health, Education, and Welfare Secretary John W. Gardner has said: "We have a great and honored tradition of stumbling into the future. In management of the present, our nation is—as nations go —fairly rational, systematic, and orderly. But when it comes to movement into the future, we are heedless and impulsive. We leap before we look. We act first and think later. We back into next year's problems by studying the solutions to last year's problems."

Bertrand de Jouvenel has written that the 20th century now has the opportunity to devise "a long-term strategy for well-being." As I read the Preamble to the Constitution, it seems to me that this was precisely the goal of the 18th century Constitutional Convention. Today, a vigorous program—backed by the collective political wisdom of the Congress and the technical expertise of the social scientists —finally offers us hope of achieving that goal.

June 1968

The Case for
A National
Social Science Foundation

Social science has had its foot in the door in Washington for some time, but now it stands a chance of getting its head in, too. Bills are pending in both the Senate and the House to establish a national foundation for the social sciences. The pages that follow indicate the range of testimony on S.836, the bill introduced in the Senate by Senator Fred Harris (D., Okla.). Harris is also chairman of the subcommittee on Government research of the Committee on Government Operations, and it was this subcommittee that held hearings on S.836 in February and June of 1967. A companion bill has been prepared by Rep. Donald M. Fraser (D., Minn.)

Senator Harris's staff is optimistic about the chances for the new foundation to be approved; the Senator himself is taking the tack that more money and recognition for the social sciences are not luxuries, but necessities. As he said in introducing the bill, "Man can accomplish so many things these days—not excluding world devastation—by merely pushing a button; we understand the button and the machine very well, but we are woefully weak in understanding the button pusher."

In the beginning, at least, the new foundation would do more for the visibility and influence of social science in Government than it would for social research. But this greater visibility and influence might end situations like those described by Herbert A. Simon of the Carnegie Institute of Technology: "Social scientists are . . . being handed problems whose physical, biological, and engineering aspects have been 'solved' and then being asked to take care of unwanted social and psychological consequences."

The endowment of the new foundation would be modest. Senator Harris has written into the bill a first-year authorization of $20 million. The National Science Foundation, out of its $480 million total, is already budgeting more than $40 million for the social sciences. The National Institutes of Health spent $39.5 million on social-science research this year. In all, the Federal Government will spend $314 million for social research in fiscal 1967. Of that, $239 million will be done by outside researchers. *All* Federal research—including research in natural science and about $2 million for the National Foundation on the Arts and Humanities—totals more than $5 billion.

Much of this research—in all fields—is nuts-and-bolts work, needed by an agency to do its job. The Department of Agriculture budgeted about $27.9 million for social research, the great part of which goes for studies of marketing, crop processing, and agricultural production—Agriculture alone accounts for about two-thirds of all Federal research in economics. The Department of Health, Education, and Welfare plans to spend $176.8 million for social science, much of it concentrated in applied studies in the Office of Education, but about $40 million to be spent in more basic research through the N.I.H. The Department of Labor devotes about $10 million annually to social-science research. The department allots $2.1 million for basic research, most of which goes for studies in labor statistics. The State Department spends about $5.5 million supporting social-science research and study abroad, most of it spent on the East-West Center in Honolulu. The department's Bureau of Intelligence and Research has an annual budget of some $4 million and produces about 1000 formal research papers and another 1000 informal responses to queries from within the Government. Its director, Thomas L. Hughes, characterizes this research as "more what serious journalists would produce if they had the time."

Much of the research done by the intelligence bureau is classified, of course, as is much done by the Department of Defense and other intelligence, security, and defense agencies. In some cases, the very existence of the research is a secret. The C.I.A. may produce more social-science research than all the rest of the Government, but no one really knows. (One informed estimate gives the C.I.A. about 13 percent of the 8000-plus social scientists employed by the Federal Government.)

S.836 prohibits the proposed foundation from doing classified research, but the original version did provide that the foundation could carry out up to one-fourth of its research at the request of Government agencies willing to provide the funds and relinquish control of the research. This provision was sharply criticized during the hearings, and Steven Ebbin, staff director of the subcommittee, reports that it will either be left out of the bill entirely or such research limited to nonsensitive agencies. Other changes in the bill, Ebbin reports, are that it will "carefully and forcefully spell out" that the new foundation should support training and education of social scientists, and that the foundation will be permitted to do research on the "state of the art" and on its own progress in supporting social science.

The bill itself is a windfall from the storm that accompanied the fall of Project Camelot. But the idea of massive Federal support for the social sciences has been around since the end of World War II. At that time, social scientists were clamoring to be included in the planned National Science Foundation, and they were included—under the umbrella heading, "the other sciences"—when the N.S.F. was established in 1950. Since the confusion between social science and socialism was particularly popular in those days, the backers of social science were willing to take what they could get. The *Journal* of the Americal Medical Association voiced a typical complaint against *any* inclusion of the social sciences: "The social sciences are themselves so young and their techniques at present so experimental and poorly controlled as to indicate some doubt as to whether or not their development has proceeded sufficiently to warrant incorporation in the proposed agency." Another professional group opposing inclusion of the social sciences was the engineers, but their point—in 1945—was that "the social sciences are important enough to be placed under a special roof."

Today the N.S.F. subsidizes a vast range of social research, but most witnesses before the committee maintained that its concentration is on the "scientific" wing of social science.

Although the hearings can be considered an exercise in macrograntsmanship, the social scientists who appeared were unfailingly frank in telling the senators that social-science research is bound to be controversial. As John Buettner-Janusch said, "It is very disconcerting and sometimes terrifying to read an anthropological or sociological account of one's own community." This prospect frightens the *New York Times* as well. "Could social scientists financed by the proposed foundation really work in freedom from fear of Congressional reaction to unpopular conclusions they might reach?" the *Times* asked. Harris, however, believes that social-science research can withstand criticism—and without the protective umbrella of the National Science Foundation.

This suggestion, that the social sciences might fare better under the N.S.F., emerged as one of the key points of the hearings. Harris's hope is that a new funding agency for the social sciences will promote more diversity in Federal research. And neither Harris nor anyone else expects the N.S.F. or the N.I.H. or any other agency to cut back on social-science spending on account of the creation of a new foundation.

However, none of the Government witnesses—even those favorable to the social sciences—made any distinction between giving more money for social-science research to the N.S.F. and giving more money to an entirely new foundation. This was apparently the result of a decision on the part of the Bureau of the Budget against supporting S.836. However, the Bureau has now been impressed by the support shown for the new foundation and is reconsidering its opposition. Perhaps the most significant co-sponsor of the bill, after all, is one who joined during the hearings— the former head of the speech department and a social-science instructor at General Beadle State Teachers College, Madison, S.D., a formidable fiscal conservative, Senator Karl Mundt (R., S.D.).

Senator Harris, it might be added, is himself by no means an enemy of natural science or the National Science Foundation. In fact, this fall he led a successful floor fight to add $20 million to the N.S.F. budget for fiscal year 1968 over the $480 million budgeted in fiscal year 1967.

The testimony below has been edited and condensed in order to present a picture of the concerns of the witnesses in a limited space. The full text is available from the subcommittee.

PUBLIC UNINTEREST IN SOCIAL SCIENCE

W. Willard Wirtz

I have tried to suggest what seems to me the issue before the committee by referring to the classic and now very tired statement of H.G. Wells: "Human history becomes more and more a race between education and catastrophe." My guess is that the text is still very good, but the times have very much changed the emphasis.

I am frankly not sure any longer, and I say it at the risk of being misunderstood, which side education *is* on. It seems to me that catastrophe may actually be the consequence of the disparate outcome in the race between two kinds of education—one in the physical sciences and the other in the social sciences. I believe that physical science may get so far out in front of the social sciences that a catastrophe may result.

I should like to emphasize that the present development of research in the social sciences falls so far short of its potential, and the necessity for its infinitely larger development, that our problem is actually one of whether there are ways to express a recognition of the problem. I have tried to grope for an understanding of something that, as I say, is so far beyond what we are presently doing that I am not even sure about the tools with which I am working.

I want to make it quite clear that this is not meant, in any way, as a criticism of the present scholarship in this field or of the present administration of it.

But I believe that there is a very definite limiting factor, and we might as well face it squarely. I believe that this limiting factor is a very real doubt in democracy's mind—but not in that of its antagonists—whether it really *wants* any further expert advice in the science of human relationships. For this is peculiarly an area in which every single one of us thinks he is an expert. And if he is not enough of an expert, he would rather play it by hunch than try to find out what somebody else's expertness might imply.

I do not believe it is much exaggeration to say that the present attitude toward social science—*real* social science—is just about the same as the prevailing attitude toward the physical sciences at that point in time when people looked and saw that the sun "comes up" in the morning and "goes down" at night and said, "Let us not bother any more about it."

Now, that type of mistake was so pervasive that it still characterizes our whole discussion about the social sciences. We got over that mistake, as far as the physical sciences are concerned, and moved forward several centuries ago—and particularly in the last 50 years—to a point where, instead of feeding the physical scientists hemlock, we suddenly elevated them to so high a pedestal that we are perfectly willing to recognize that they know a lot more about their area than we can possibly know. We have almost given up trying to keep up with them. And when they invent a new communications satellite, which involves consequences of infinite importance to the whole human race, we turn our franchise over to a corporation and just forget about the whole thing.

Now, we must not be tempted to do that as far as the social sciences are concerned, even though Kenneth Boulding of the University of Michigan—who always seems to me to identify what is just a little ahead of us faster than almost anyone else—has written:

"There seems to be a fundamental disposition in mankind to limit agenda, often quite arbitrarily, perhaps because of our fears of information overload. We all tend to retreat into the cozy, closed spaces of limited agendas and responsibilities, into tribalism, nationalism, and religious and political sectarianism and dogmatism."

IMPROVING FEDERALLY FUNDED RESEARCH

Dankwart A. Rustow

Let me sum up my objections to some of the current methods of Federal financing of social-science research.

Suppose that some recent international crisis has drawn the Federal Government's attention to the country of Ruritania. In due course, the head of some Government office—who has not the time to ferret out or read the half-dozen scholarly articles on the politics of Ruritania—approves a $250,000 research project on the subject. Contract specifications are then drawn up by minor officials in the procurement division, officials who have little notion of how research is conducted or knowledge obtained.

The money appropriated might pay the salaries of 10 first-rate specialists on Ruritania for two years— but it turns out that there are only three such specialists in the entire United States. And precisely because they are good scholars, they hold tenure positions at leading universities; can obtain private-foundation funds for their research; and hence lack any material incentive to take on a Government contract. Because they are good scholars, too, they are apt to feel repelled by the naive concepts and the clumsy jargon of the specifications.

The contract, therefore, goes to a second-rate or third-rate institution and to scholars who have little competence in Ruritanian politics. The additional staff that inevitably must be recruited will have even less competence. And whatever the research procedures followed, the results are likely to be far below normal scholarly standards. If some of the researchers are sent abroad, they will, in addition, make a bad name for American social science—and hence impede the work of the three bona-fide Ruritania specialists on their next trips to the field. With a bit of ill luck, they will complicate the task not only of social science but of American diplomacy as well.

If my picture is correct, it seems clear that no

amount of reviewing of contracts by officials in the State Department's Bureau of Intelligence and Research will safeguard against these dangers. On the contrary, the additional paperwork and negotiation involved is likely to keep good scholars further away from Government projects.

Let me emphasize that the evils I see are not caused type of procedure that I have tried to describe. The dangers can be avoided, and opportunities for high-quality research can be maximized, I believe, by adopting three principles for all Government-sponsored basic research in the social sciences.

■ The initiative for the formulation of research projects must come from the scholarly side.

■ The allocation of funds for research proposals must be in the hands of groups of people who are themselves well-qualified social scientists and experienced researchers.

■ There should be an emphasis on projects by individuals, by small groups, or by established institutions, rather than by far-flung organizations set up *ad hoc*.

I hasten to add that there are several programs under military or partially military sponsorship that have, in effect, worked on those principles in the past—the work of the Russian Research Center at Harvard, of the Center of International Studies at the Massachusetts Institute of Technology, and of the Social Science Division of the RAND Corporation being prominent examples. These organizations have consisted of first-rate scholars; their work has not been dependent wholly on Government funds; and their prestige has been such that, in any negotiations for contracts with Government agencies, it was their collective scholarly judgment—rather than some uninformed bureaucratic judgment—

that could prevail. But I submit that these have been rather exceptional cases, and that the operations and vicissitudes of Project Camelot have perhaps been more typical of what one has a right to expect of militarily-sponsored social science.

A "MAJOR STEP" IN AMERICA'S PROGRESS

Fred Harvey Harrington

In reviewing the February testimony before this committee on S.836, and the hearings last summer on international science and behavioral research, I was struck with the feeling that, in many respects, the social sciences are today where the physical and biological sciences were in the late 1940s. At that time my predecessors in the presidency of the University of Wisconsin—Edwin B. Fred and the late Conrad Elvehjem—came here to plead for the creation of the National Science Foundation.

They described, for example, how university scientists had labored for years in fundamental studies of the atom—useless information at the time—and how in the dead of night in World War II, after the possible application of this "pursuit of knowledge for its own sake" had been recognized, Wisconsin's atom smasher was moved from the campus to Los Alamos. They called for postwar rebuilding of the "stockpile of basic scientific knowledge" that fuels economic and industrial progress and improvements in public health. They complained that Government agencies—conscious of their legal goals—concentrated their grants in problem-solving studies and areas where fast answers were needed. They warned that this was short-sighted, that the Federal Government was responsible for building both the strength of the scientific community and the store of fundamental knowledge, and that if this was left undone the nation would suffer. Science must have a spokesman at the highest administrative councils, they said. The need for fundamental studies must be understood and funded.

My points to you today are virtually the same—but for the social sciences.

As long as there have been scholars in history, economics, political science, sociology, communication, and the other social studies, there has been fundamental research in these areas. All major universities in America recognize the distinctive characteristics of the social sciences and tend to hold them together in recognition of their status with the biological and physical sciences, the arts and the humanities. In some respects they are the bridge between C.P. Snow's two cultures, the reason why American universities do not have the great, impassable chasm he so dramatically described.

That we look today to the social sciences for answers to our problems of poverty, international development, urban sprawl, and all the other social, economic, and political ills that man is heir to is evidence enough of the importance of the social sciences to the nation. But the pressing nature of these problems has developed public impatience with the scholar who says, "We must know more about man and his institutions and interrelationships before we can come to long-range solutions."

Obviously, in the physical and biological sciences, as well as in the social sciences, both applied and fundamental work must go on simultaneously. A national foundation for the social sciences can make this possible, as did the National Science Foundation.

There are some who contend that these things could be accomplished within the present Federal structure—that social sciences, as half-brother to the natural sciences on the one side and to the humanities on the other, could prosper. It is too early in the life of the National Foundation for the Arts and Humanities to ask that it produce some evidence of fair treatment of its half-brother. But the N.S.F., sincere in its efforts to spread its concern into the social sciences, has not yet proved, with a $21-million expenditure, its effectiveness in invigorating fundamental social studies.

There are some who contend that the creation of a third foundation would destroy the unity of knowledge or impair the interrelationship of scholars in the various fields. Quite the contrary, it would remove a source of irritation and improve interrelationships and interdisciplinary research efforts. There is no one so irrationally irritating at a family reunion as a poor relative. Raising the status and the funding of the social sciences would enhance the unity of knowledge.

There are some who contend that adding another foundation would fragment Governmental support of fundamental research. And it would—to the benefit of all. It would place in the hands of a social-scientist administrator and a board of social scientists a considerable amount of responsibility for the progress in the social sciences. There may be some evil in this, but it is nothing compared with the suspicions spawned when this responsibility falls upon an administrator who is a physicist and a board heavily weighted with physical and biological scientists, regardless of their good intentions.

There are some who contend that establishment of a foundation for the social sciences might reduce the support from other Federal agencies for social-science research. This is possible, and may also be helpful. The creation of the N.S.F. reduced appreciably the "bootlegging" of fundamental study support into project work in the natural sciences. The creation of a social-science foundation could be expected to have similar results. And this could bring some reason and regularity into the whole field of Federal research support.

I do have a recommendation for change in S.836, a change I consider extremely important.

Americans like to see quick results from expenditures of tax dollars, and I don't blame them. We ask a great deal of our people. But by its very nature, a national foundation for the social sciences will not produce quick results. And by the modest appropriation proposed, the possibility of major, fast advance through the studies it supports is extremely limited.

The expenditures for social-science studies at the University of Wisconsin are currently about $8 million a year. With this volume of work, we produce few spectacular findings. Thus I would strongly recommend that you raise the fiscal sights of this bill to a point so that significant, early progress is likely. My personal feeling is that this could be accomplished with an annual appropriation of $500 million at the start, with a provision for raises over the years at the rate of about 10 percent a year.

This is a small percentage of our nation's annual investment in the *repair* of social damage. Prevention is always cheaper than a cure.

In addition, I see in the creation of a national foundation for the social sciences a major step in the progress of America toward a good life for all its people and an approach to world peace and fellowship. We should not quibble when the goals are of such magnitude.

WHO USES U.S.-SPONSORED RESEARCH?

John M. Plank

Government-sponsored research in the social sciences that is done on the outside can be ranged along a number of spectra. The principal spectrum is the one running from basic research at one end to something not far removed from spot intelligence at the other. And it is with that spectrum that I want to deal here.

In terms of content, it is impossible to draw a hard-and-fast line between intelligence and research, a fact given implicit recognition in the very title of the State Department "Bureau of Intelligence and Research." A good social-science research product will contain much valuable intelligence material, and a good spot-intelligence report often contains information of substantial research value.

As seen by the U.S. Government, both intelligence and research reports are designed for the same end-users, the policy-makers, to help them function better. As seen by the outside research world, however, the distinction between intelligence and research is felt to be a real one, intelligence being somehow unsavory, arcane, vaguely pernicious, and research being the opposite of these things.

I believe the research community is profoundly mistaken about the nature of intelligence and that it should reexamine its attitude. On the other hand, the propensity of those in government to classify their data as secret, to force outsiders who would deal with these data to go through elaborate rites of initiation—clearances, interrogations, and briefings—and, in general, to divide the citizenry into "insiders" and "outsiders," discourages really effective communication and cooperation between the two worlds.

In any event, it seems to me that classification is carried much too far, and that most of the outside research in the social sciences presently contracted for by individual Government agencies could be supported—more efficiently, more effectively, and less hazardously—by a single national social-sciences foundation. This is emphatically true of such massive basic-research projects as the unfortunate Camelot; it is true, also, in my view, of most studies of groups, institutions, and trends. Two points in this connection:

■ I strongly suspect that the ideas for most external research projects do not originate inside the funding agencies, but on the outside. Sometimes a full-fledged project proposal will be submitted by an outside researcher to a potential funding agency inside government. Sometimes the idea for a project will emerge during a conversation between a Government representative and an outsider. Sometimes a Government officer will come across the germ of a research project in his reading of what in the State Department is called "collateral" material—anything not prepared under official auspices. I suspect it is in such ways that most external research projects originate, rather than through intensive in-house planning.

My judgment is that a well-staffed, alert national foundation for the social sciences would elicit as good, or better, research proposals in as great, or greater, quantity from the outside-research community as the individual Government agencies do today. My further judgment is that those projects, when carried out, would prove to be of as great, or greater, usefulness to the operating agencies as the products of the present system.

■ I think we need to ask what use is now made inside government of the products of external social-science research. Who reads the results of this research? Who makes policy on the basis of an understanding of it? There are, as we know, mountains of such research in the State Department, the Defense Department, the Central Intelligence Agency, and elsewhere. My own observation is that comparatively little use is made of it—partly because most of it does not lend itself to direct and immediate policy proposals, and partly because people in policy-making positions in government simply do not have the time, the energy, or even perhaps the background to assimilate it and draw operationally useful conclusions.

What I am suggesting is that much of the present external-research product is not being fully exploited. And I think it is likely that shifting the source of funding for basic research in the social sciences, and publishing all such research, would not radically affect either the policy-making machinery of government or the nature of the policy made. Indeed, much research of potentially great usefulness to Government policy-makers is already being done by scholars independent of Government support altogether.

*   *   *

THE NEED FOR "DANGEROUS TRUTHS"

Irving Louis Horowitz / Herbert Blumer

Congress has to concern itself with what may be an already dangerous imbalance between too much policy-oriented research and too little basic research. The legislative branch must take into account the fact that, even in advance of its creation, there is an impulse to view a national social-sciences foundation as a means to strengthen the hands of those who look upon the social sciences as simply national security resources. I think that Congress should see to it that the creation of still another agency does not give rise to the sort of unholy alliances that at times are established between virtually autonomous Federal agencies and the entrepreneurial empires scattered throughout the world of social science. It is a worthy objective that such an agency be neutral and not policy-oriented.

I don't think it is too early to search for answers to the problems that may immediately confront such an N.S.S.F. In the briefest possible way, we should like to examine at least a few of these. Doubtless, the committee will understand that these observations and queries are intended to be supportive of an N.S.S.F., since the encouragement of basic research in the social sciences is vital to the health of American society.

The nature of the social and behavioral sciences makes the sort of consensus about methodology and goals, which exists in the natural sciences, highly unlikely at this time.

Not in contention here is whether or not one chooses to describe the social sciences as continuous and contiguous with the natural sciences, or sharply breaking with the "non-human" sciences. It would not be the N.S.S.F.'s function to answer such conjectural matters, nor would its function be to hang too many research pegs on any one approach now fashionable. But such an organization should support studies to assist in settling these long-standing debates as to the proper nature and proper subject matter of the various sciences.

Turning to another matter, the conduct of basic social-science research deeply and directly affects policy issues and political sentiments. What is required is an appreciation that intellectual and ideological sensitivities are involved, and they cannot be ignored. To convert the meaning of pure social science into an operational codebook for noncontroversial social science would be self-defeating and even, in my opinion, suicidal.

There are already social-science organizations supporting nonsensitive research—such as the Twentieth Century Fund and the Bollingen Foundation. What should be encouraged by Congressional legislation is research into dangerous areas. The oversimplified identification of social science with natural-science techniques may lead away from this search for dangerous truths. Granting agencies should *not* assume that a noncontroversial and accommodating style is equivalent to a maximum yield in substantive findings.

We have a tradition, inherited from the feudal world, of *noblesse oblige* and of being very kind to one another because we live in a world in which words are, in our special breed of intellectual cats, equivalent to fists. We tend to be overly sensitive, needlessly solicitous, and as a result we tend not to be as intellectually sharp with one another as we ought to be.

The formation of an N.S.S.F. would involve a higher concentration of organizational energies, intellectual talent, and financial sources than has hitherto ever been the case in the social sciences. It is therefore extremely important that social-science research facilities be strictly maintained on a pluralistic basis. Care should be taken to prevent the multiple forms of social-science research from being smothered or obscured by the development of a monolithic agency committed to a single, limited orientation.

We should encourage Congress to stimulate both the various policy-making and non-policy-making agencies to use basic social-science research findings and to originate social-science projects within legislative and executive agencies. The creation of an N.S.S.F. should be an occasion for vitalizing research services of existing organizations, not for demoralizing them. From the poverty program to the Pan-American Union, efforts to generate independent social-science research must be redoubled.

It would be easier to stimulate basic social-science research through an independent institution, such as an N.S.S.F., than to simply allocate more funds for policy agencies. The fact is that existing Federal departments are concerned, most of the time, with fostering special ends of their own rather than with the autonomous goals of the social sciences. Furthermore, there would be a strong foreign resistance to any work commissioned through an N.S.S.F. that had a direct policy commitment. The findings generated by a policy-oriented N.S.S.F. would more nearly represent an official line than anything now done by social scientists working under Federal grants or contracts. To avoid this possibility, the independent character of any

N.S.S.F. must be guaranteed as far as possible by legislative safeguards.

Such an organization should not be allowed to become a centralized research center that encourages consensualist responses and conforming research designs. These bureaucratic tendencies are not calculated to improve the breed of the social sciences. In any pluralistic democratic society, a certain strain between science and policy is not only inevitable but valuable.

This strain may provide a sounding-board of hard truths against which policy-making must echo its sentiments. American society would be far weaker if its policy decisions were exclusively guided by, say, public-opinion polls than by the gamut of social-scientific data now in use. To convert the proposed N.S.S.F. into an adjunct of policy is to run a grave risk of undermining its independence. This potential loss of intellectual nerve can easily occur when other avenues of Government financing of social-science research projects become narrowed. The creation of a new agency of social research should, therefore, be used to inform existing agencies of the need for basic social-science findings in the conduct of their own work. Not to do so may create a one-sided imbalance favoring present policy-research agencies over and against basic research requirements.

A "NEED FOR INCREASING COHESION"

Leland J. Haworth

The National Science Foundation was established in 1950 to foster and encourage basic research and education in all the sciences. At that time, it was not clear to the Congress or to others how far the Foundation ought to go in the social sciences. From the legislative history, it is clear that Congress felt that the Foundation itself ought to determine how fast and how far it should go.

In 1953, the Foundation began a study of a possible program in the social sciences comparable in every way to the ones in the natural sciences. The Foundation's first social-science program was approved in 1954. At first, support of the social sciences was confined to those areas that "converged" with the natural sciences. In 1956, however, the social sciences were given separate identity—the social-science research program was created, consolidating research support from all divisions and eliminating the criterion of "convergence."

In 1960 the Social Science Division was established, placing the social sciences on the same administrative level as the other divisions that existed at that time: biological and medical sciences, and mathematical, physical, and engineering sciences.

The social-sciences division, of course, was initially very small. It has grown in the last six or seven years much more rapidly than the Foundation's program as a whole. Since 1960 it has doubled. The fractional part of the Foundation's research funds that it represents is now growing at a rate of 15 percent or 20 percent a year. For the current year, it has reached a bit more than $20 million.

For the social sciences in 1968, we have requested an increase of not quite 25 percent. But we can't clearly spell the rest of our support for the social sciences. These other funds represent composite and varied support. I have in mind such things as our providing matching funds to assist universities in constructing buildings for their graduate programs, and our investment in education, including fellowships, teacher training and retraining, curriculum development, and undergraduate-research participation. You can never predict how the benefits will be distributed among natural science, social science, engineering, and so forth.

Our support goes clear across the spectrum of the social sciences. Initially not all disciplines were covered, but I think it is fair to say that all are covered now and that the proposals in any branch of the social sciences are welcome.

One important point should be noted. For some disciplines, such as archaeology and the history and philosophy of science, the Foundation has been practically the sole source of Federal research funds; for other disciplines, such as political science, economics, linguistics, and demography, the Foundation is the major source of basic, non-mission-oriented work.

In describing the Foundation's social-science research program and our criteria for it, let me first discuss two broad legislative boundaries that circumscribe the program and that are inherent in the Foundation's mission. First, all our research programs in the social sciences at the present time must be "basic" in nature. Second, they must be "scientific." (The National Science Foundation Act of 1950 authorizes the Foundation to initiate and support "basic scientific research.") The Foundation interprets this language broadly, however, and encourages a variety of research approaches to a wide range of subjects, including research projects that are problem-oriented—so long as the research promises to yield valid scientific generalizations, rather than find solutions to problems peculiar to a particular time, place, or event.

Nevertheless, certain areas of social-science research

are, at the present time, denied Foundation support. Applied or professional clinical studies are not eligible. This excludes the larger part of social work, clinical psychology, legal studies, and a very large percentage of overseas research that is primarily applied in nature. Applied social-science research, however, is supported by the Department of State, the Arms Control and Disarmament Agency, and the Peace Corps.

Fortunately, the percentage of research in social sciences that meets the criterion of being scientific has been growing. Experience has shown that although techniques of investigation may vary among different branches of social science, the spirit of objective and analytical inquiry is common to all. There is every reason to hope that patterns and regularities observable in the social scene will become increasingly amenable to objective analysis and ultimately to statement in the form of scientific laws.

The specific criteria that we apply in our support of basic-research projects in the social sciences are those that offer the best combination of encouragement for the advancement of human knowledge—combined with suitable safeguards against undesirable duplication, exceeding the bounds of legislative authority, and violation of standards of scholarly excellence and sound judgment.

I should say that, in common with all the Foundation's programs, the initiative for deciding what an individual is going to do research on really comes from him. We don't go out and tap people on the shoulder and say, "We would like you to do this kind of project or that kind of project," but use our influence in a general way.

I would like to turn now to a fairly broad statement

of the sort of thing we visualize for the future. We have given a lot of thought to this in the last year or two, and we were stimulated to further thought by the considerations that you and your committee have been giving to the social sciences.

We need to give additional support to centers for advanced specialized research, particularly those engaged in attacking multi-disciplinary problems. Some of these centers lead a precarious financial existence, and finding resources inevitably wastes professional time. We believe there needs to be a rationalization of their organization, financial basis, regional dispersion, and specialization, for they will shape research in the future even more than they have to the present.

The social sciences now have only one center of a national character—the Center for Advanced Study in the Behavioral Sciences at Stanford. The Center affords senior scholars a place to pursue advanced research or to write up research results away from their normal academic environment. A national center for social-science research located in Washington is also a recurrent theme. Certainly Washington contains vital material—both archival and living—that is inadequately exploited.

It is important that we expand also our support of basic social-science research in the underdeveloped world. At the present time, a wide range of disciplines are involved in comparative studies of social, psychological, economic, and political topics in Asia, Africa, and Latin America. All share a concern in understanding the problems of developing countries. There is, as yet, little coordination of these efforts.

We would like to help develop regional basic-research centers where the prospective overseas researcher would receive appropriate intensive training to supplement his own disciplinary competence. For example, an anthropologist could learn about the political structure of the country; a political scientist could learn about the social structure. Both groups might require special language training, whereas a linguist might require knowledge about the most appropriate ways of approaching natives.

In a different context, we propose to increase support for a special class of projects—to develop sets of methods or models for demonstrating new powers of analysis. Recently, a small number of individuals, organized as the Mathematical Social Science Board, developed a class of mathematical models that have brought new insights and approaches to bear on social-science training and research programs. The pattern is flexible and can be adapted to various levels of difficulty and to the needs of several social-science disciplines.

Now, all of these things can be done within the N.S.F.'s present authority. If our authority were broadened, we could increase our effectiveness. We have in mind authorization to undertake what could be called, in general, "applied research."

One example would be programs to bring social-science knowledge to social practitioners, such as local officials, police officers, social workers, and clergymen. We would also like to see social-science research incorporated into Federal, state, and local welfare programs—not just at the planning stage, but in the execution as well. A third area of extension we have considered is a combination of social-science engineering and natural sciences to attack technological problems, such as water and air pollution, the pressure of population, and the inadequacies of mass transportation. However, the time has come when we must move beyond the facile identification of promising research opportunities.

In addition, the National Endowment for the Humanities and the Foundation have agreed to establish cooperative arrangements for the joint support of projects straddling the spheres of responsibility of the two agencies.

Finally, I come to a position on the bill that you introduced, Senator Harris. First, I would like to say that although I am going to register a serious doubt about it, I recognize fully that it is a matter of opinion and judgment. It is one on which reasonable men can disagree, and a difficult thing to prove in either direction.

There is no question that a separate foundation for the social sciences would give the social sciences more visibility. Just the fact that a foundation of that name existed, dedicated to the social sciences, would have that effect. It might prove to be a center of intellectual stimulus. It would certainly provide another source of general funding. Whatever might be the net result in *total* funding, it would be done from a different, but not necessarily better, standpoint from that of other agencies.

On the other hand, we feel that there are serious difficulties, or potential difficulties, of which I believe the strongest is that there is a great need for increasing cohesion in this whole spectrum that I have been talking about. I have never believed that the two cultures are as sharply divided as our good British friend, C.P. Snow, expressed it, but I believe that there has not been enough mutuality of interest, not enough common viewpoint. Incidentally, this gap exists *within* the natural sciences and *within* the social sciences, as well as between the natural sciences and the social sciences and the natural sciences and engineering, and all of these and the humanities. There has not been enough integration, enough recognition, enough across-the-board scholarship and interest among these disciplines.

My principal concern about a separate foundation for the social sciences would be the splintering effect that it might have.

My second objection relates to the effectiveness of the Government operations in themselves. I question whether a separate agency is good from this standpoint. It certainly would have some drawbacks. I am wondering whether the advantages would be enough to make up for these drawbacks.

Now, I hasten to add that I am not saying that the Government agencies now engaging in social-science research should *not* be engaged in such research. But I do question whether there should be one agency engaged in the development of the underlying knowledge and understanding that the mission-oriented agencies as well as other public and private agencies need to help advance society and overcome some of its difficulties.

For there is some danger that, if a separate foundation were established, many of the more basic research programs of mission-oriented agencies and the N.S.F. would be viewed as redundant, with consequent cutbacks or limitations in their funding.

*   *   *

THE ARGUMENTS FOR AND AGAINST

Launor F. Carter

In the paragraphs that follow, I wish to consider a number of arguments in favor of the proposed foundation, as well as to comment on several that are used as arguments against the foundation.

Social scientists' aspirations need raising.

As has been well documented, most of the support for research and advanced development has been given to the physical and biological sciences. Social-science scientists have generally not aspired to the level of support required to develop the basic knowledge that can lead to a frontal attack on the many social problems facing our nation. Generally, social scientists have worked as single individuals and as part of the university academic departments, doing research within the limited resources available for small studies. They have been traditionally content with limited resources for individual study, for travel to collect data, or for relatively minor experimentation.

This limited attack on the various basic problems in the social sciences is not sufficiently productive; large, well-financed, and carefully organized projects must take the place of small, individual efforts. Social scientists will make this transition to project research only if they believe that sufficient support is available to undertake such efforts.

Social scientists need spokesmen who will present their needs and aspirations to the Administration and to Congress.

Within the present organization of the Office of

Science and Technology, the National Science Foundation, the research establishment of the Defense Department, and the Department of Health, Education, and Welfare, there are no social scientists who hold responsible senior positions *and* have as their mission the presentation of the case for extensive social-science research. While there *are* social scientists holding senior positions on some of these agencies, they are not primarily devoted and dedicated to furthering the cause of social-science research; their orientation is to the overall mission of the agency. Since the social sciences are so comparatively less well developed and understood than the physical and biological sciences, it is important that their needs and potential receive relatively greater support than some of the other scientific and research areas.

Better people need to be attracted to the social sciences.

It is often asserted that the better people are attracted to those areas of scientific specialization where there is great national interest and where resources allow them to undertake the kinds of studies that will make important contributions to intellectual understanding.

Recent material published by the Educational Testing Service shows that the natural sciences and social sciences attract equally good students as far as verbal aptitude is concerned, but the social-science students are significantly low in quantitative ability. I believe this lack of numerical aptitude hinders the development of a true research-based social science.

The level of funding for the social sciences needs to be radically increased.

Generally, the level of support for the social sciences

is between 5 percent and 10 percent of the level of support in other scientific areas. The total level of Federal support for social sciences is around $325 million, with over half representing funds coming from the U.S. Office of Education for research in education. In 1966, the N.S.F. supported social-science activities to the extent of $29.7 million out of a budget of $466 million, or 6.4 percent.

In this respect, it is important to note that the N.S.F. lumps together all of the social sciences: Economics, political science, sociology, anthropology, social psychology, and so on, go into one category to arrive at the $29 million. But in the physical sciences each one is treated separately: Mathematics receives $45 million, physics $50 million, chemistry $40 million, astronomy $24 million, and so on. In other words, the level of support of social science, considered collectively, was less than that of a number of other single disciplines in the physical sciences. It appears that we put our major support in those areas where our understanding is highest, rather than in those where it is lowest and needs the greatest improvement.

The cost of experimental social-science studies is high and increasing.

It is often argued that social-science research is relatively inexpensive. Once this was the case, but modern empirical social-science research, if properly done, *is* expensive. Empirical social science depends on the collection and extensive analysis of data. At times it involves experimental manipulation, which—if done in real-life situations—is quite expensive. The cost of collecting survey information on any large representative population runs into thousands of dollars. Maintaining of large data banks by modern information-processing techniques costs hundreds of thousands of dollars a year.

Historical and theoretical social science needs support.

At the present time, there are only modest sums available to support social-science research that is oriented toward empirical investigations. But there are only *minute* funds available for the support of those social scientists whose orientation is essentially historical and theoretical. Their ability to obtain such simple things as adequate library support, clerical support, or even time away from their teaching duties is often very limited.

As the committee is well aware, there are a significant number of social and natural scientists who oppose the formation of a separate social-science foundation. I would like to consider two of the arguments they commonly advance.

Good ideas in the social sciences receive adequate support now.

It is often argued that, under the current levels of funding, any social scientist of repute who has good ideas receives adequate support. There is some truth to this, and it represents a contradictory dilemma regarding the social sciences.

It is true that many social scientists are being supported by the N.S.F., the N.I.H., and the Defense Department. This funding is at a level that is reasonable, in terms of these scientists' current needs and current conception of the support needed to perform social-science studies.

I would argue, however, that this is a result of the fact that for many years social scientists received next to no support, and thus were unable to plan or think in terms of experimental work truly adequate to the phenomena they were studying. There are many important theories in the social sciences having to do with delinquency, crime, housing, urban affairs, social organization, disarmament, and so forth, that have never been attacked with the vigor and intensity they should be attacked with—because funds were simply not available to allow researchers to undertake a long-range, intensive study of these areas.

Science should not be divided.

There are those who contend that it is unwise to set up a separate foundation for the social sciences—on the grounds that the N.S.F. has established a Social Science Division, and is giving increasing support to this division. Further, with adequate support from the Administration and Congress, the N.S.F. will increase its attention to this area.

My experience with the N.S.F. indicates that all of this is true, and that the director and deputy director have the best of intentions regarding the support of the social sciences. Nevertheless, the N.S.F., with its historic orientation in the physical and biological sciences, cannot furnish the dedicated and focused leadership the social sciences need. The social sciences need their own protagonists in the highest levels of Government, simply because the development of a powerful understanding of our social problems is a matter of the first importance.

In addition, it is sometimes asserted that the social sciences, the biological sciences, and the physical sciences should all be under the same roof, since they represent the totality of the scientific discipline. To the extent that this argument is based on mere propinquity, it does not stand careful scrutiny. The contribution of the physical and biological sciences to most social science is relatively small, since most of the social sciences are relatively unrelated to the new developments or new advances in the physical and biological sciences.

In summary, Mr. Chairman, it is my belief that the arguments in favor of the establishment of a national social-science foundation greatly overweigh the arguments opposing such a foundation.

January/February 1968